Syndicalism, Industrial Unionism, and Socialism

by John Spargo

Red and Black Publishers, St Petersburg, Florida

First published by BW Huebsch, 1913

Library of Congress Cataloging-in-Publication Data

Spargo, John, 1876-1966.
    Syndicalism, industrial unionism, and socialism / by John Spargo.
        p. cm.
    Originally published : BW Huebsch, 1913."
    ISBN 978-1-934941-67-6
1. Syndicalism. 2. Socialism. I. Title.
    HD6477.S7 2009
    335'.82--dc22

                                                            2009020824

Red and Black Publishers, PO Box 7542, St Petersburg, Florida, 33734
Contact us at: info@RedandBlackPublishers.com

Printed and manufactured in the United States of America

Contents

Preface

In December, 1912, and January, 1913, by invitation of one of the Brooklyn branches of the Socialist Party, I delivered a series of five lectures on Syndicalism. Some of the lectures I repeated in a number of other places.

It had long been in my mind to discuss some of the more important phases of Syndicalist philosophy and tactics from the point of view of a Marxian Socialist who holds to the policies of the international Socialist movement, so that the invitation to deliver the lectures was welcome because it afforded a convenient opportunity for fulfilling my plan.

By way of introduction to this little volume, I cannot do better than add to the foregoing account of its history the brief apologies with which I prefaced the first lecture.

"As will presently appear, I am not a believer in Syndicalism. Much of my life has been spent in combating its principles. For that reason I shall be the more careful to keep all taint of partisanship from my statement of its principles and aims, however much I may afterward assail them. I trust that the statement of the Syndicalist position which I shall make will satisfy most thoroughly of all the thoughtful Syndicalist, who knows just why he is a Syndicalist, and is not merely a victim of the glitter of new phrases. I shall impute nothing to my Syndicalist friends which is not frankly set forth in their own literature. My own interest, not less than theirs, requires a perfectly true and balanced account of the essentials of Syndicalism and a disregard for non-essentials imposed upon it by individual idiosyncrasies. This is not easy of attainment, for Syndicalism is in the formative stage. Its doctrines are not fully developed, its philosophy is rather chaotic. But I shall try to state the case for Syndicalism more clearly and consecutively than has yet been done in English, with a determination to be scrupulously fair.

"To attain this result a sympathetic understanding of the movement is essential. So I shall try to view it, not with the cold detachment of the entomologist dissecting a beetle, but with the sympathetic interest of one dealing with a life which he has closely touched and shared. For I have faced the same problems as my Syndicalist brother, shared his struggles, his hopes and his fears. For I am of the proletariat, bone of its bone and blood of its blood. Strike, lockout, blacklist, overwork, unemployment, homelessness and hunger are all familiar phenomena to me. I have borne them in my person. They have shaped— and marred—my life. No Syndicalist has seen more clearly the difficulties, obstacles and dangers of parliamentary Socialism. I have both preached and practiced sabotage. I have looked with awe and fear upon the long road of pacific evolution by political methods, and found my courage and faith taxed to the uttermost. At such times I have listened with eager and hungry heart to the Siren voice offering an easy way to the shores of the Promised Land. Sometimes I have almost decided to follow the call. So I feel that I can understand those who decide to try the way of 'direct action.' The Siren's form is fair and her voice is sweet. But she is a Siren, nevertheless, and those who follow her call are doomed."

My thanks are due to the good comrades who arranged for the delivery of the lectures in Brooklyn. I have many pleasant memories of the live evenings and trust that some of my friendly auditors derived as much pleasure and benefit as I myself did.

John Spargo

Old Bennington, Vermont.

January, 1913.

What Is Syndicalism?

The definition of new movements is proverbially difficult. Whenever a new movement appears, or an old movement enters upon a new phase of its development, the issue between the old order and the new is generally distorted. Hence controversies arise, and the controversial temper impairs the mental vision. Exaggerated claims are made by the friends of the new order, exaggerated fears expressed by the defenders of the old.

This truth is illustrated at the present time by the furious discussion of Syndicalism, which is a new development of an old movement, challenging us with problems which appear new though they are in reality only old problems in a new dress. The stormy discussion is as reckless as the autumn gale that strips the trees. Definition is rarely attempted, notwithstanding that it is the greatest need of all. For no matter whether we belong to those who march under the new banners and shout the new watchwords, to the defenders of the old order who cling to the battle-stained banners and shout the old watchwords, or to the greater host of wavering and undecided souls, we all need a clear and authoritative definition of the issues and problems involved in the conflict. The most important step toward the determination of any controversy is its proper definition.

The word "Syndicalism" is, in popular usage, the French equivalent of the English term "trade unionism." In English the word "syndicate" is used to describe a combination of capitalists to promote some particular enterprise or speculation. In France the word is more widely applied and denotes any association of persons formed to promote special interests held by those comprised in the association. Thus our English term "trade unionism" is translated into French as *"syndicates ouvriers,"* that is, syndicates, or associations, of workers. Etymologically, therefore, the French word *"Syndicalisme"* connotes the system or policy of any kind of syndicate. But in popular use it is applied almost exclusively to labor unionism. We may say, then, that Syndicalism is only the French name for labor unionism.

It is very obvious, however, that outside of France the word is not used as a synonym for labor unionism, at least, not the labor unionism with which we are all familiar. If it means labor unionism to us it must mean a particular type of unionism, essentially different from the type we have long known. For the most ardent labor unionists are the most bitter enemies of Syndicalism and are, in turn, most abused by the Syndicalists. What is the explanation?

In transplanting the word *"Syndicalisme"* to the English vocabulary we have neglected the adjectives with which it is associated in France. There, standing by itself, it connotes the simple fact of unionism. But in France, as elsewhere, there are unions and unions. Some unions are conservative. Their policies are characterized by moderation and a tacit recognition of the equal rights of employers and employees as parties to a bargain. Other unions are radical. Their policies are aggressive and characterized by a fierce insistence that the employers are parasites, and that the interests of the workers alone are worthy of consideration. The former are sometimes designated "yellow" and sometimes "conservative." The latter are sometimes designated "red" and sometimes "revolutionary". In our English use Syndicalism always refers to the "red" or "revolutionary" form of labor unionism.

II.

The aims of labor unionism of the type with which we have long been familiar are fairly well defined, and easily understood. Either by specific declaration or by implication, it accepts as a fact the division of modern industrial society into classes with antagonistic interests. Its existence is the result of a conviction that the employers as a class do not and cannot have the same interests as the wage-earners, and that the wage-earners must combine, in order that by their collective power they may wrest from their employers higher wages, shorter hours and improved conditions of labor. This philosophy is shared by the most conservative as well as by the most radical labor unionists. Apart from it labor unionism could have no *raison d'être*.

Either by specific declaration or by implication, too, all unions, whether radical or conservative, accept the view that the laborer is exploited; that the sum of rent, interest and profit is produced by the addition to natural resources of human labor (using that term as all the great economists do to include all forms of productive effort) and should belong to the laborer. The enjoyment of this sum by others is the result of a parasitic extortion which ought to be eliminated.

Some of the unions make radical declarations of these principles in their membership pledges and constitutions. They declare that there is a fundamental conflict between the capitalists and the workers which can only end when the system of exploitation through the medium of wages is destroyed. Other unions may refuse to adopt such declarations of faith and even repudiate them, avowing their desire to be only "a fair day's wages for a fair day's work" and for harmonious relations with their employers. But in actual practice this theoretical moderation is of little or no consequence. Ask any organizer belonging to such a union to justify the existence of his union, and he will at once begin to argue that the worker needs it to protect himself against encroachments on his liberty or standard of living by the employer. Ask him why such a danger exists if the employers' interests are not contrary to the interests of the workers, in their special relations as employers and employees, and he will at once surrender his union's declared faith and fall back upon its real faith, which is rooted in the stern realities of class conflict.

Ask such an organizer to define what is meant by "a fair day's wages for a fair day's work," to state the principle or principles by which it is to be determined, and he will be forced to admit that the phrase is really meaningless. What he really believes is that the workers get as much as they can compel the employers to pay, and that they ought to struggle to make the employers pay more and more for less and less work, until the logical end is attained and nothing is taken from labor as rent, interest and profit.

The unions are generally organized upon craft lines. The historical reasons for this fact are obvious and well-known and need not be discussed at length. Masons organized as masons, carpenters as carpenters, shoemakers as shoemakers, and so on, each craft union adopting rules and methods corresponding to its own needs. The craft unions, in other words, were born of historical and economic necessity. Of course, there were always trades which were closely related, as, for example, the tanners and the shoemakers, and from the very beginning of trade unionism the logic of necessity has led to plans and efforts to unite the unions of such related trades. Sometimes the plans and experiments have taken the form of the federation of autonomous craft unions with joint rules and a common working policy. At other times it has taken the form of the amalgamation of several craft unions into one general union covering the related crafts.

It is trite to say that many modern discoveries are really re-discoveries, but it is well to bear the fact in mind and to remember that what we today call "Industrial Unionism," and regard as a new discovery, has a history almost as ancient as trade unionism itself. Even in 1834, at the first national congress of trades unions ever held, it was the most discussed issue of the day! Seventy years ago the coal miners of Great Britain were attempting to combine in one great union every person employed in or about the mines, no matter in what capacity.

But historical development rarely pursues a straight course. There are many tortuous windings. Side by side with the centralization of trade unionism, through the merging of local unions into national unions, and the federation of craft unions, a process of decentralization which was quite as important took place. This, too, was due to historical and economic necessity. While some industries have been entirely absorbed by other industries, in other cases industries have been so highly specialized that what were formerly branches of an industry are now separate industries. To correspond with this movement in industry, we find re-alignments and re-formations of trade unions, so that there are several craft unions in place of a single union, just as there are several trades in place of one.

This specialization and division in turn has led to such a degree of industrial interdependence, and to such complexity, that craft unionism is rapidly becoming an anachronism, especially in those industries in which machinery is the chief force. Thus we see the evolutionary process to be dualistic. What was at first a single trade union, embracing all the members of a given industry, was transformed, decomposed into several small craft unions, perhaps as many as a dozen, or even more. That decomposition was not the result of the acceptance of a false theory, but of the development of industry itself. But that development continuing reaches a point at which it forces the unions, not to further division and disintegration, but to amalgamation and re-integration. No Marxian Socialist can be surprised that the forms and the policies of the unions are always adjusting themselves to accord with the development of industry itself, rather than to accord with theories.

The characteristic weapons of labor unionism are the strike and the boycott. Political action, by which I mean parliamentary action resulting from the use of the ballot, is sometimes included. The sense of class solidarity developed by unionism leads naturally to united political action for the attainment of certain ends through legislation. Thus union labor parties have arisen in many countries. But the weapons which are peculiar to labor unionism, inherent in its very nature, are the strike and the boycott.

Now, if we consider these weapons carefully we at once observe that they are very different in one important respect. The boycott has never been of any great value when attempted by the workers in a single craft. The strike, on the other hand, has often been of immense value when attempted by the workers in a single craft. To illustrate: Suppose the workers in a big shoe factory to be on strike for better conditions, and their places filled by non-union workers. The workers decide to declare a boycott against the shoes produced in that factory. It is obvious that if the boycott is to be practiced only by the strikers and their families it will not amount to very much. But if all the unions join in the boycott and refuse to purchase the shoes produced in that factory, the boycott may become a very formidable weapon. The boycott is essentially a class weapon rather than a craft weapon. Of course, class solidarity has often caused it to be used by the class for the special benefit of the craft, but that is, for the moment, beside the mark.

On the other hand, the strike has been, in the main, a craft weapon. As such it originated. Shoemakers went on strike, that is, refused to work until their demands were met, but weavers and masons were unaffected and so kept at work. Sometimes workers in closely allied crafts went out on strike from sympathetic motives, the tanners, for example, striking to help the shoemakers to win. That was the logic of economic necessity. When craft unions federated, as in the textile trades, to cite a notable example, the same logic made the strike an industrial one. On the other hand, when the single union of a trade was decomposed into a number of smaller unions, the strikes of these newer craft unions became less effective. The sense of class solidarity was weakened by the disintegration. In proportion as the units represented smaller proportions of the whole work of production, their group interest flourished at the expense of their class interest. Clinging to old methods and traditions, each union caring for itself, making terms for itself, striking by itself, it came to pass that in the event of a strike by one group of workers in a factory, the task of filling their places was less difficult than if the entire force had to be replaced. The other workers, members of other unions, could remain at work and feel themselves absolved from the stigma of "scabbing," for they were loyal union men, loyal, that is, to their own unions, and were living up to the contracts made by their unions.

This condition has resulted in a great weakening of craft unionism as a method of class warfare. It has fostered sectionalism, faction fights and the warfare of union against union. It has also been a potent breeder of treachery by trusted leaders and officials. A single craft union, by the simple device of a contract extending over a long period of time, or terminable only after a certain long notice, can make it difficult and perhaps impossible for any of the unions of related crafts to strike effectively. Quite recently, when the stereotypers made common cause with the pressmen employed on the Chicago newspapers, and joined their strike, the local union of stereotypers was expelled from the national body on the ground that it had violated a contract with the employers by going on strike. The local members of the International Typographical Union were prevented from joining the strike by the threat of a similar punishment, made by the international officers, for the same reason.

Thus sectional union contracts have come to be relied upon by the capitalist class as one of their very strongest safeguards.

It is not without interest to note in this connection that the British trade unions, though they still suffer greatly from this evil, have been steadily and quietly working towards its elimination for many years, by aiming to have all union contracts made for the same period of time and terminable on the same date.

III.

Syndicalism aims, among other things, to abolish these evils of craft unionism. It is a product of the inevitable revolt of an element in the labor union movement which vehemently opposes to the ideals of craft solidarity the ideal of class solidarity. It is possible to sympathize fully with the aim while rejecting the methods proposed for its attainment. By no means are the opponents of Syndicalism all to be classed together as being opposed to its ideal of class solidarity. Many of them are working to that end within the existing unions, and oppose the Syndicalists on the ground that their policies retard the normal development of class as opposed to craft unionism.

Syndicalism is best described as a movement rather than as a social philosophy. There is a sort of Syndicalist philosophy, to be sure, but it is as a movement that it is most important. The methods of Syndicalism—like its theories—differ somewhat in different countries, as we shall see, but there is sufficient unity of aim and method to warrant a composite picture of the whole body of theories and methods as a description of Syndicalism in general. For our present purpose, Syndicalism may be defined as follows:

Syndicalism is a form of labor unionism which aims at the abolition of the capitalist system based upon the exploitation of the workers, and its replacement by a new social order free from class domination and exploitation. Its distinctive principle as a practical movement is that these ends are to be attained by the direct action of the unions, without parliamentary action or the intervention of the State. The distinctive feature of its ideal is that in the new social order the political State will not exist, the only form of government being the administration of industry directly by the workers themselves.

Here or there may be found a Syndicalist to whom some part of this definition may not be acceptable, for Syndicalism is in the process of making, as it were, and is for that reason not capable of rigid definition. On the whole, our definition will probably be acceptable to the vast majority of Syndicalists.

It will be seen that Syndicalism is primarily an amalgam of Anarchist and Socialist theories. The class struggle, which the Anarchists logically deny, is a fundamental principle of Syndicalism. The necessity of political action and the conquest of the State by the proletariat, which Socialists affirm, the Syndicalists deny. The self-sufficiency of "direct action," which the Anarchists have long preached, is the cornerstone of Syndicalist policy. The municipalization and nationalization of industry, which is everywhere a central demand in the Socialist programme, Syndicalism rejects completely with utter disdain. There is a much greater amount of Anarchism than of Marxian Socialism in the Syndicalist amalgam! But there is another element in the amalgam, namely, trade unionism. The chief weapon of Syndicalism, the principal form of "direct action " is that weapon which is characteristic of trade unionism and without which trade unionism could not have existed, the strike. It is quite an interesting study to observe how the most reactionary of old-fashioned labor unionists and Syndicalists arrive at the same practical result. Believing in the sufficiency of trade unionism, relying completely upon the strike and the boycott, the old-fashioned unionist denies the need for political action. He points to the fact that certain trades enjoy the eight-hour workday, for example, won by the union and not brought about by legislation. The Syndicalist takes the same attitude and defends it by the same argument. Extremes meet!

As a rough classification it may be said that philosophically Syndicalism is based upon the Socialist doctrine of class warfare; that its ideal is derived from the Anarchist propaganda and that its weapons are the weapons of trade unionism — whetted and polished upon the whetstone of Bakuninism.

IV.

All Syndicalists agree that in the new social order toward which they are striving the political State will have no place. There is complete agreement that the only government which will be necessary will be the government of industry, of production and distribution, and that this will be carried on directly by the workers themselves. There is not the same degree of unanimity concerning the organization which is to take the place of the State; the manner in which the ideal of industrial government is to be attained. This is quite natural and inevitable, and no Marxian Socialist will attack the Syndicalists because they do not present an inflexible dogma concerning the future organization of society.

In France, the home of revolutionary Syndicalism, the prevailing theory is that in place of government by a political State there will be simply an economic administration by the *syndicats*. The union is regarded as being at once the superior fighting force of today and the germ of the economic administration of the coming social order. Edouard Berth and Emile Pouget, skilled literary propagandists of the movement, take this view, and from their writings one gets an idea of something like a revival of the medieval guilds. The functions of the union at present, according to the Syndicalist, are (1) to fight against capitalism continually, by any method available, and (2) to educate its members in every way and to prepare them for their future role and its responsibilities. This education must be many-sided. It must include education upon social problems, especially social organization, which is essential if the workers are to reorganize society. It must include industrial education, particularly in improved technical methods and processes, for that is essential if the workers are to prove competent administrators of production. It must include, also, the general culture of the workers for their own satisfaction as individuals, as well as for the general elevation of society.

In the future, the functions of the unions will be (1) to act as productive groups, and (2) to act as units in a federation of unions which will organize production and regulate consumption, and administer the general social interests. In the words of M. Pouget, "In the future it will be the base on which the normal society, purged of exploitation and oppression, will arise." Sorel, the greatest intellectual exponent of the movement, has expressed a very similar view in his pamphlet, *L'avenir Socialists des Syndicats*, as also has M. Edouard Berth in his writings. Berth is essentially a disciple of Proudhon and has advocated a form of unionism in which the guild is closely copied. There are three degrees of rank; first the apprentice, second the journeyman, third the master. Official sanction was given to the theory that the labor unions in the various industries will, in the new social order, manage the industries, by the leading Syndicalist body, the *Confédération Générale du Travail*, at its convention in 1906, when it was declared that "the fighting groups of today will be the producing and distributing groups of tomorrow."

Now, in all this there is nothing new. It is, on the contrary, quite old. Whether we consider it as a survival or as a revival, we cannot regard it as other than old. For example, I turn to the history of the International Workingmen's Association and find most of it clearly expressed. Thus at the Congress of 1869, held at Basle, a Proudhonian delegate advocated the concentration of the energies of the International upon the formation of unions or *syndicats*, first because "they are the means of resisting exploitation in the present," and, secondly, because "the grouping of different trades in the city will form the commune of the future," when "the government will be replaced by federated councils of *syndicats,* and by a committee of their respective delegates regulating the relation of labor — this taking the place of politics."

At this point, I venture upon a digression to interject the observation that a good deal of the confusion and panic which the Syndicalist agitation has wrought in the ranks of the Socialists of England and America result from unfamiliarity with the history of the Socialist movement. This ignorance has made it possible for very ancient and discarded ideas to be accepted as new. About a year ago, I sat in the office of the Socialist mayor of a large city and listened with mingled amusement and surprise while my comrade, the mayor, with a patronizing tone reproached me for my neglect of and indifference to the "new ideas" which he had recently discovered. Of a small group of Socialists, myself among the number, he said, "You have stagnated. You have lost touch with the realities of life. Devoted to the movement and fighting for it, you have not had time to develop intellectually. There are new ideas which none of you have recognized, though they are the ideas which dominate the real movement. Mere political Socialism is outworn. Political action was once our sole weapon: now there are greater weapons. The new Socialism is concerned with Industrial Democracy, a new conception. We shall not need the State, the workers industrially organized will rule society. That is Industrial Democracy, but whoever heard of it, or of the General Strike or of Industrial Unionism, until lately?" My comrade was rather astonished, and, I have no doubt, quite skeptical and unconvinced, when I told him that these "new ideas" were quite old; that the idea of autonomous industrial groups displacing the State was a pet idea of Proudhon's followers half a century ago; that Robert Owen anticipated the ideas and methods of the Industrial Workers of the World in detail four score years ago, and that the General Strike was one of the "chestnuts" of the old International in Marx's time.

Some of the Syndicalists are quite frank in their recognition of these facts and present Syndicalism as a revival of Owenism and Proudhonism rather than as a new movement. Thus Tom Mann, the British Syndicalist, in an article entitled *Syndicalism at Work*, written while he was serving a term of imprisonment for his "seditious speeches," specifically claims that Syndicalism is but a revival of the Owenite agitation:

Syndicalism means the control of industry by "Syndicates," or Unions of Workers, in the interest of the entire community; this necessarily pre-supposes the relatively perfect industrial organization of all who work, and the right relationship to each other of every section. Robert Owen, over eighty years ago, advocated the necessity for such a method of organisation, and made a very good start at putting it into practice; but, as it proved, the workers were not equal to resorting to such relatively highly-trained methods; and the workers have had to spend twice forty years in the industrial wilderness because they were neither mentally nor physically qualified to enter the "promised land." Several other methods have been resorted to by the workers to escape from their industrial bondage since Owen's time, but none of them have proved really effective, Parliamentary action least of all.

> In Robert Owen's vigorous days the workers of England had no political "rights," and it would appear that Owen set small store by the possession of any such "rights." He saw and taught that the workers' difficulties arose as a consequence of their industrial subjugation to the Capitalist class— in other words, that the Employing class had no concern for the working class, except to control and exploit their labour force for the specific purpose of using them as profit-making machines for themselves.

An editorial article in the English Anarchist journal, *Freedom*, gives equal credit to Proudhon and Robert Owen as co-founders of Syndicalism. Proudhon, in his *L'Idee Générale de la Revolution*, declared the real revolutionary aim to be "to melt, to merge, to dissolve the political or governmental system into an economic one by reducing, simplifying, decentralizing, and abolishing one after the other all parts of the enormous machine called Government or State." *Freedom* expresses the hope that the newly started English Syndicalist movement may meet "the same success as was enjoyed by the Owenite movement at that period [1834], when the Owenite General Union of Productive classes had more than 500,000 members, among whom were many agricultural laborers' unions as well as working women's organizations." Of course, such a membership was claimed for Owen's great industrial union at the time, but it is very well known that it was not a real membership in the sense in which that term is used by the unions of today with their systematic membership fees. The historians of English trade unionism remind us that "as no discoverable regular contribution was exacted for central expenses, the affiliation or absorption of existing branches was very easy." Moreover, all who in moments of great enthusiasm at public meetings had declared sympathy with the movement seem to have been regarded as members.

How completely Owen anticipated the teachings of Haywood and other leaders of our I.W.W. a brief statement of his views will show. He believed that a non-political combination of the wage-earners could raise wages and shorten the hours of labor "to an extent which at no very distant time would give them the whole proceeds of their labor." We are told that:

> "Under the system proposed by Owen the instruments of production were to become the property, not of the whole community, but of the particular set of workers who used them. The trade unions were to be 'transformed into national companies' to carry on all the manufactures. The agricultural union was to take possession of the land, the miners' union of the mines, the textile unions of the factories. Each trade was to be carried on by its particular trade union, centralized into one grand lodge."

The great social revolution was to be accomplished very swiftly. Owen himself thought that six months' time would be sufficient. By an automatic process the whole capitalist organization of industry was to be replaced by an organization of industry by the unions. Not only were the aims of Owen similar to those of the revolutionary Syndicalists of today, but his methods were equally similar: the same tactics were preached— low membership fees, industrial organization, "one big union," the General Strike and obstruction of industry were all advocated and practiced.

In the editorial already quoted, *Freedom* declares:

> "But Proudhon's Mutualism, as well as the Owenite movement, were diverted from their economic action by political movements, as, for instance, Chartism. This will not be the case with Syndicalism, with its direct action against Capitalism and the State. To act against the State means to attack, to destroy its political institutions, and to substitute for the State organization the Industrial Unions of the producing classes."

So much for our digression: I remember discussing, years ago, the subject of the French labor movement and the peculiarities of its development with that veteran Socialist, Lucien Sanial, and a very illuminating observation which he then made. Speaking of the prevalence in France of Proudhonian ideas and their persistence there long after they have disappeared from other countries, he suggested that in France generally, but especially in Paris, the intellectual center, industries are still largely carried on in workshops, each with a few journeymen under a master workman, and that this fact explains why the view prevails that the society of the future will be based upon autonomous industrial groups, and the persistence of Anarchistic conceptions generally. Since then the same explanation of Syndicalism has been suggested by Sombart in his *Socialism and the Social Movement*. Certainly the French Syndicalist ideal reflects French industrial conditions. From the point of view of the industrial development of

Germany, England or America it seems grotesque and reactionary.

V.

Outside of France, Syndicalism has made its most rapid and substantial progress in Italy, where economic conditions are more like those of France than any other country. Of the twenty-five million of Italy's adult population ten million are employed in agriculture. It has its peasant proprietors, only the less prosperous of whom work for wages, and then only occasionally. Many of them are French-speaking, particularly in the upper Aosta valley. It has its *metayer* system, especially in Tuscany and Lombardy, under which the people are relatively prosperous. Under the *metayer* system the landlord provides the land, a share of the capital and the tenant supplies the rest of the capital and the necessary labor. Thus, a landlord may supply the land, the necessary cattle, vines, olives, trees or seed and the tenant the labor and necessary implements. At harvest time they share in the results, being equally benefited by good harvests and equally injured by bad harvests. This system was once quite common in England and this country and "farming on shares" is even now not wholly unknown. In the neighborhood of the large cities tenant farmers employ wage laborers whose conditions are often miserable in the extreme. Finally, there are forms of cooperative agriculture which are peculiar to Italy. Land is owned by small groups and either by the group as such or in individual plots but with collectively-owned implements, and the products collectively marketed. The manufacturing industries are in general more nearly like those of France than those of Germany or England.

Naturally, the organizations of the workers reflect these conditions. The unions are very numerous, very poor, very unstable and generally local in their character. There is a loose federation of the unions of agricultural workers and a rather stronger federation of the unions of industrial workers. Cooperative societies of all kinds are common. They are generally local, confined to a single village or town. There are cooperative banks, cooperative stores, cooperative associations of carpenters, bricklayers, and so on.

It is not surprising, therefore, that the ideal of the new society held by most of the Italian Syndicalists is very similar to that of their French brethren, with rather more emphasis upon cooperation. Thus, Arturo Labriola, whose position as the intellectual leader of Italian Syndicalism is universally admitted, takes the view of the union as the unit of industrial and social administration held by Pouget, Sorel, Berth and other French leaders. The unit can be only "an association of the workers who already possess the technical capacity necessary for managing production." It is rather startling to find this Syndicalist suggesting as a means of transforming society the union competing for contracts against ordinary capitalists, becoming in fact an immense cooperative concern, doing for its members all that the State now does, but doing it more efficiently; educating the children, caring for the aged, attending to matters relating to health and sanitation, in a word, taking its members and their families away from the care and direction of the State. Thus, Labriola argues, the State would simply cease to be. He even suggests that the unions might borrow the capital of the capitalists and pay a rate of interest agreed upon! At this we hold our breath. But Signor Labriola is only temporising, we find. As soon as the unions are strong enough, and closely enough federated, they can refuse to pay any more interest or to return the principal. Thus the revolution will have been peacefully accomplished. The capitalists will have to work and their special directive gifts will immensely facilitate production.

There is, perhaps, less bitter hostility to political action in Italian Syndicalism than in that of France, but it is growing in volume and intensity. Almost grudgingly, Labriola and Enrico Leone admit that political reforms may be of some help, particularly in breaking down class privileges which are based on legal sanctions. But it is "direct action" which is all important. The power of the capitalist class does not reside in the State, they say. The State is at most one of the means of maintaining a power whose real source is the economic unpreparedness of the workers. To prepare themselves, by unions and by cooperation — that is the need, and that is the way to freedom from class tyranny.

VI.

There is very little Syndicalism in Germany, the "*Lokalisten*" unions are few and small and their influence quite inconsiderable. Their views are substantially those of the French Syndicalists. There is very little Syndicalism in England, despite a popular notion to the contrary widely prevalent in this country. As in Sweden and Denmark, it is confined to a small but noisy group, and draws its inspiration chiefly from the French Syndicalists and the Industrial Workers of the World, which is the American Syndicalist movement. What little Syndicalism there is in England takes the American view of the importance of the organization of unions on industrial lines rather than the French view which extols spirit rather than form. That is a natural result of the greater similarity of industrial development which exists between England and America. On the other hand, the English Syndicalists follow the French in their attitude toward existing unions and oppose the I.W.W. policy.

American Syndicalism, as represented by the I.W.W. is distinguished from European Syndicalism by its policy toward the existing labor unions and its theories of union organization. Like the French and Italian Syndicalists, the Industrial Workers of the World are violently opposed to the State and seek to supplant it by a labor union administration. Typical are the utterances of William D. Haywood, as reported in the New York *Call* and *Volkszeitung*, "I despise the law " — " No true Socialist can be a law-abiding citizen," — " When the worker comes to know the truth . . . he will use any weapon to win his fight, therefore he does not hesitate to break the laws." — "Under Socialism the government will be an industrial government, a shop government." Like their French and Italian brethren, these American Syndicalists laugh at political action, or "parliamentarism" and rely upon direct action. "The tactics used are determined solely by the power of the organization to make good in their use. The question of 'right' and 'wrong' does not concern us," says Vincent St. John. "The principal weapon is the strike, and when that fails to force concessions from the employers, work is resumed and 'sabotage' is used to force the employers to concede the demands of the workers." "In short, the I W.W. advocates the use of militant 'direct action' tactics to the full extent of our power to make good."

Like their fellow Syndicalists in Europe, the Industrial Workers of the World declare themselves to be neither specifically Socialists nor specifically Anarchists, but simply revolutionary workers. There are no political tests. Whether a man calls himself a Socialist or an Anarchist, a Christian or an Atheist, or whether he be a native citizen or a foreigner, is not considered. The only test for membership is "does he work for wages?" So far good and well. The theory is admirable. But in actual practice the I.W.W., like all Syndicalist organizations, is anti-political, and carries on a warfare of special vigor and bitterness against the Socialist Party. While it turns to the Socialist Party for financial aid at all times and to its elected representatives for support, its rules provide that no local union shall, under any circumstances, contribute funds to the support of any political organization, Socialist or otherwise. I shall return to this one-sided arrangement, the parasitical relation of Syndicalism to political Socialism, later. For the present it is enough to note that the I.W.W. is an anti-political organization.

Having noted the main points of identity between the Industrial Workers of the World and European Syndicalism, let us now consider the one important difference. We can best do that by a brief statement of the history of the I.W.W. The salient facts are all contained in a small pamphlet by Vincent St. John, *The I.W.W., Its History, Structure and Methods,* which is published by the I.W.W. itself and is, therefore, an official record.

VII.

In the autumn of 1904 six men active in the labor union movement, most if not all of them being Socialists, met in conference and discussed the conditions prevailing in the labor movement, especially the abuses and weaknesses arising from craft unionism. As a result of their deliberations, they agreed to invite a number of others to a further secret conference, which was held in Chicago in January 1905. Thirty-six persons in all were invited, only two of whom declined to attend. At this conference a Manifesto was drawn up and ordered to be published. This Manifesto set forth the familiar criticism of craft unionism and the American Federation of Labor and the need of a new type of organization, and called for a convention to be held in Chicago in June for the purpose of launching such an organization. This convention met and adopted a plan of industrial unionism. All the workers engaged in one industry in any locality, according to the plan adopted, must be organized into a local union of that industry. Thus, in any particular factory there would be no rival unions in conflicting craft lines, but one homogeneous unit of organization. All such local unions of a particular industry are to be combined into a National Industrial Union with full jurisdiction over the whole of the local unions of that industry. National unions representing closely allied industries are in turn to be combined into Departmental Organizations. Thus, the National union of bakers would combine with the National unions of butchers, grocery clerks and so on, into the Department of Food Products. Finally, all these department organizations are to be combined into the General Organization, and this in turn provides the unit of International Organization.

The ideal of the I.W.W. is thus accurately enough expressed in the popular watchword, "One Big Union." This is not, of itself, contrary to the ordinary trade union ideal. It is as old as trade unionism itself. Students of the history of English trade unionism will recall many attempts at its realization. It was heard in 1828. In 1834 the cry was for "industrial amalgamation" and a bold and serious attempt was made to unite all the workers employed in the seven different building trades into one National Builders' Union instead of seven craft unions. In 1844, and again in 1863, a similar effort was made to form one great union of miners. In the same period repeated efforts were made to unite all the workers in the iron trades. The idea was preached by men like William Newton, who founded the Amalgamated Society of Engineers, and is indicated by the name he gave that society. It was his hope to include in one great national union every engineering mechanic. That these schemes all failed was not due to their defects as schemes, but to the fact that they did not prove to be the most efficient forms of organization. The unions took the forms determined by industrial conditions.

The founders of the I.W.W. were pure utopians. They set up an ideal and said, ""Let us make a movement in keeping with our ideals." The important truth that labor organizations, like other institutions, are shaped by economic conditions, adapting themselves to changes in economic conditions, was lost sight of. They saw within the existing movement a very definite tendency toward industrial organization manifest itself, not as a result of contemplating a beautiful theory, but in response to the needs revealed by daily contact with reality. The miners, the brewery workers, and others were evolving industrialism within the existing movement, but the I.W.W. could not trust to the evolution of the existing unions — probably because so many of its leading spirits were not bona fide workers but intellectuals. With typical utopian impatience and disregard of evolutionary forces, it began a new organization, entered into rivalry with the American Federation of Labor and added to the disunion and strife of the labor movement.

In this the I.W.W. took a course directly opposite to that of the French and Italian Syndicalists, who have taken great care to avoid the formation of dual organizations and have relied upon the evolution of the existing unions. They have sought to develop the unions already formed, permeating them with Syndicalist ideals, only attempting to form new unions for those workers for whom provision is not already made. I can best illustrate the difference of method by supposing that at the time of the formation of the I.W.W. the spirit of the French Syndicalists had prevailed. Then, instead of the strong radical minorities withdrawing from the various unions, leaving them in the hands of the reactionary masses, they would have remained in their unions and kept up their work as militant minorities, inspiring and educating the mass to the revolutionary view. They would not have withdrawn. The minority within the American Federation of Labor which, loyal to the unions at all times, is striving to bring them to the acceptance of the industrial form of organization is, therefore, acting in harmony with the French Syndicalist example.

VIII.

As a result of the methods of the I.W.W., a new Syndicalist organization has been formed, the Syndicalist League of North America. Its methods are those of the French and Italian Syndicalists, and it is most outspoken in its criticism of the I.W.W. and its utopian theories. Its membership is small, but its propaganda is characterized by a greater grasp of the problems of social and industrial organization than is that of the larger body, the I.W.W.

Tom Mann, the English Syndicalist, takes the same view as will be seen from the following extract from an editorial article in *The Syndicalist*, September, 1912:

> "If the opposition of the A.F. of L. should make the continued life of the I.W.W. impossible, then there is the remedy by which both capitalists and politicians can be defeated by rejoining the A.F. of L. Unions, and taking up the work with the men inside in order that a militant minority can expound and propagate the Syndicalist ideas and methods."

Equally with the I.W.W. and the French and Italian Syndicalist organizations, the Syndicalist League advocates industrial unionism, that is, the organization of the workers by industries rather than by crafts. But it differs from the I.W.W. in that like the French Syndicalists, it regards the form as of less importance than the spirit of the organization. A craft union with a revolutionary spirit is far better, from this point of view, than an industrial union which has not the revolutionary spirit. But that is not all: the League is opposed to the "One Big Union" idea as preached by the I.W.W. It is opposed to the centralization of power which is the distinctive feature of the I.W.W. and advocates decentralized industrial unionism, that is, local industrial unions with full autonomy. Like the French Syndicalists the members of the League fear that the outcome of centralized power cannot be other than industrial despotism. They point to the fact that the great *Confédération Générale du Travail* in France is a typical decentralized Syndicalist organization, composed of craft unions and industrial unions, loosely federated, with complete autonomy, no union being compelled to surrender its autonomy to any governing body of the confederation. Solidarity is a spiritual quality wholly independent of forms.

The League points out that the I.W.W. form of organization which denies autonomy to local unions and centralizes power in the hands of a national executive, really involves the ideal of bureaucratic government in the future society. For the I.W.W. ideal of the operation and management of industries by the workers employed in them, the mines by the miners, and so on, must be considered in conjunction with the ideal of industrial organization, and the "One Big Union" with its central authority. This, say the Syndicalists, of the League, means authoritarianism and bureaucracy. It means the creation of a despotic industrial State in place of a political State. In the very nature of things, they say, the industrial State to which the I.W.W. plans must logically lead would be less elastic, less capable of affording personal freedom, than the present political State. If all the unions are to be centralized in one big union and its power centralized in the hands of a single authority, can the government of society by that union be other than bureaucratic?

IX.

We have now, I think, a fairly definite picture of the Syndicalist movement and its aim. Whether we take the Syndicalism of Labriola, of Sorel or of Haywood, of the *Confédération Génerale du Travail*, the Industrial Workers of the World or the Syndicalist League of North America, we find that they are all agreed upon the following principles:

(1) Capitalism is to be destroyed and with its must be overthrown the political State.

(2) These ends can only be accomplished by the working class itself.

(3) They are not to be obtained through political action, but as a result of the direct action of the workers, (that is, as direct results of economic conflict not indirectly by means of legislation).

(4) Society is to be reconstructed by the workers and economic exploitation and mastery will be abolished.

(5) In the new Society the unions of the workers will own and manage all industries, regulate consumption and administer the general social interests. There will be no other form of government.

We are to consider the principal weapons of Syndicalism and its methods of warfare later on. For the present it is only necessary to guard against a misconception of the term "direct action." There are numerous confusions and controversies as a result of a lack of careful definition of the terms used. Socialists fight each other savagely because they mean different things by the terms used. "Direct action" is used by some as a synonym for violence, for assaults on the person and destruction of property. The mad acts of the McNamaras and their associates in blowing up buildings are regarded as typical forms of "direct action." So defined, "direct action" is very vigorously condemned. But there can be no sense in assailing a man as an "advocate of arson and murder" if by "direct action" he does not mean anything of the sort. And that is what is done, unfortunately. Men who use the term "direct action" to cover a policy that is entirely pacific and legal are classed with dangerous criminals of the McNamara type.

The Syndicalists are themselves to blame: they ought to have avoided the use of a term which historically is identified with insurrection and with terrorism generally, including assassination. The term has long been used by Anarchists to cover "the propaganda of the deed." alt was always so used by the followers of Michael Bakunin and John Most. The McNamaras and their confederates were engaged in "direct action" as that term has been generally understood by Socialists and Anarchists.

The Syndicalist use of the term is much more general and comprehensive. It includes violence and practically every form of social terrorism, but it includes much more. In the words of Voltairine de Cleyre, "direct action may be the extreme of violence, or it may be as peaceful as the waters of the Brook of Siloa that go softly." Any action by the workers themselves, directly, without the intervention of the State, is direct action. Thus, a strike for better wages is direct action. That is, the workers, through their own organization, without seeking legislation or State aid, aim at the desired result directly. Thus Haywood has again and again pointed to the eight-hour workday won by the New York printers as an illustration of the merit of direct action. It was gained by a strike, not by the indirect methods of political action. If a group of striking or blacklisted workers should form themselves into a cooperative association as a means of securing economic advancement, that would be direct action. Even the use of the union label is regarded as direct action. The removal of children from strikers' families to the homes of sympathetic friends in other cities, as was done at Lawrence, Mass., is also included in the scope of the meaning of direct action.

Voltairine de Cleyre, in a vigorous protest against the interpretation of direct action as meaning simply forcible attacks on life and property, cites as examples of direct action the non-resistance of the early Quakers of Massachusetts; Bacon's Rebellion; the non-importation agreements and the propaganda of the leagues for wearing homespun clothing in the period of agitation which preceded the Revolutionary War; the destruction of the revenue stamps, and of the tea in Boston harbor. She includes in her statement of the nature of direct action the numerous "free speech fights" of the Salvation Army, the Socialists and the Industrial Workers of the World; the actions of housewives in New York and elsewhere in boycotting the butchers as a protest against high prices; the work of the Grange, the Farmer's Alliance, and similar organizations; destruction of property by strikers and violent attacks on strike-breakers.

It is quite evident, then, that the term direct action covers practically every form of non-parliamentary action, the most pacific as well as the most violent, legal as well as criminal.

Granted that the man who simply believes in pacific and legal methods is foolish in applying to them the term "direct action," which is bound to convey the idea of violent and illegal methods to many minds, still, it is equally foolish for us to take the violence and illegality for granted whenever the term is used.

The principal forms of direct action are the General Strike and Sabotage, both of which we are to consider at length.

The Philosophy Of Syndicalism

I.

Having a fairly comprehensive and definite idea of the Syndicalist goal, we are naturally and inevitably led to a study of its philosophy. To understand any great social movement we must know something more than its actual programme, its goal. We must acquaint ourselves with its intellectual conceptions. We must comprehend the premises of its criticism of the existing régime and its explanation of the process by which the régime was developed. We must know, too, the principles which shape the programme of the movement, guide its policies and inspire its hope for success.

Like Socialism and Anarchism, to both of which movements it is related, Syndicalism presents itself in four main aspects, namely, (1) as an indictment of the present order; (2) as a theory of social development, including an explanation of the existing order; (3) as an ideal, a new social order to be realized, (4) as a method of attaining the goal. We must, therefore, consider

Syndicalism from each of these points of view if we want to understand its philosophy.

Now, as soon as we begin to examine Syndicalism from any one of those angles of vision we note that, with almost brutal frankness, it declares itself to be concerned only with the interest of the proletariat, the working class. This note passionately vibrates throughout its propaganda. There is a scornful disregard of all save proletarian interests. This proletarian exclusiveness is not confined to the Syndicalist indictment of the existing social order, but is the dominant note in its theory of social development, its ideal and its campaign methods. This fact gives us the first important characteristic of the Syndicalist philosophy; whatever else it may be, it is an exclusively proletarian philosophy.

We next observe that the Syndicalist attitude toward the non-proletarian element in society is not one of passive indifference merely. Syndicalism pictures the existing capitalist régime as a society composed of two great classes whose interests are fundamentally opposed to each other, and who are by that antagonism of their interests compelled to wage unceasing war against each other. This warfare is susceptible of no truce or compromise. It is war to the death, and can only be ended by the complete extermination of one class or the other. The capitalists are exploiters and oppressors of the proletariat. They have organized society in its present form for the express purpose of enslaving, oppressing and degrading the workers. Only by overthrowing the capitalist system and all its institutions can the proletariat ever hope to be free.

This is the task to which Syndicalism calls the workers. The whole fabric of capitalist society is to be destroyed and replaced by a new social order exclusively ruled by the workers—proletarians no longer, but self-emancipated, free and equal workers enjoying the full fruits of their toil without exploitation or spoliation by a parasitic class of overlords. Every wage-worker is, therefore, the natural enemy of every capitalist and every beneficiary of capitalist class rule.

The second important characteristic of Syndicalism, then, is that it is a philosophy of class warfare. It is not merely proletarian, but aggressively proletarian and aggressively anti-capitalistic. This is its bond with Socialism. Upon this rests its claim to Marxian origin and parentage. Its most able and prominent expositors claim, with much plausible reasoning, that Syndicalism is Marxism in its pure and unalloyed form. Thus Sorel, Labriola and Lagardelle, to name the three most illustrious names in Syndicalist literature, all claim to be followers of Marx, guardians of the Ark of the Covenant of Marxism. They expressly dissent from the teachings of Marx upon minor and relatively unimportant details only, and claim that Syndicalism is the only movement with a clear and indisputable claim to Marxian parentage. Parliamentary Socialism they regard as a pretender to the title.

These intellectual leaders of Syndicalism claim, furthermore, that they are engaged in the restoration of Marx's teachings to their pristine purity. Marx's followers, including even Friedrich Engels and Wilhelm Liebknecht, are charged with intellectual vandalism, with having mixed into the pure gold of Marxian theory and practical precept the alloy of bourgeois ideas and opportunistic practices. They assail belief in parliamentary action as a means of bringing about the new social order as an anti-Marxian bourgeois idea, which Engels imposed upon the Socialist movement, destroying its revolutionary character. They declare that force alone can be regarded as an effective revolutionary method. They hold that the revolutionary temper and aim of Marxian Socialism have been sacrificed to parliamentary compromise and opportunism; that the Syndicalist method of forcing a constant state of social upheaval and unrest, through persistent assaults by the proletariat on the existing social order, is the only method compatible with the revolutionary doctrines and aims of Marx; that the great Socialist parties of Europe and America have deserted the Marxian faith, and that the need of the age is for a conscious movement "back to Marx." Everywhere in the Syndicalist propaganda we encounter Marxian phrases and conceptions.

Shibboleths like "Proletarians of all countries, unite!" and "the emancipation of the workers must be wrought by the workers themselves," are claimed by the Syndicalists as their own and proudly inscribed upon their banners.

II.

In view of all this, it would be idle to deny that the Syndicalist philosophy and the philosophy of Marxian Socialism are closely related. We may freely admit so much without accepting the view that the two are identical. The Syndicalist conception of class war, if not synonymous with the Marxian class struggle theory, is a derivative from it— possibly a perversion of it.

Personally, I find it difficult to regard the claim of Sorel and other Syndicalist intellectuals that they are the restorers of Marxian Socialism, purifying it from the corrupting additions made by Engels, Liebknecht, Kautsky, and other trusted Marxists, other than as an ingenious bit of special pleading, specious but misleading. Take, for example, the claim that the parliamentary struggle of the Socialist parties is contrary to Marx's teaching and "direct action" alone compatible with it. In support of the claim it is possible to cite various sayings of Marx, hot and impatient words uttered at various times in his life, and to point to various examples of his practice. In this way quite a "case" can be made, and the brilliant intellectuals of Syndicalism have made the utmost use of the available material.

Unquestionably, Marx at various times reverted to the utopian thought-method which at all other times he vigorously assailed, and against which his entire system of thought was pitted. His whole conception of the process of social development was fundamentally an evolutionary one, diametrically opposed to the idea of the utopian Socialists that the change from capitalist society to Socialist society could be suddenly accomplished; that it needed only a revolution of force to seize the powers wielded by the ruling class, when the triumphant proletariat would proceed to the realization of their aims, the establishment of a new social order already more or less fully developed in their minds. Time and again Marx laughed to scorn this and similar crude conceptions. I need only mention here a few instances — the case of Weitling in 1847 and later; his rebuke to the Willich-Schapper faction of the Communist Alliance in 1850; his opposition, in 1862, to the mad plan of Lassalle for a revolutionary rising in Germany; and his bitter opposition to Bakunin during the last years of the "International." These examples might be greatly multiplied, but they are sufficient to establish my point.

Yet, it must be confessed that Marx at times lapsed into the very error which he so bitterly opposed. What else is his theory of the "Dictatorship of the Proletariat"? Is it not the essence of this theory that a violent revolution, a triumph of proletarian force over capitalist force, will enable the workers to seize political power, that is, the power of the State, and at once set it in motion to realize their own aims? Never in the history of the world has such an attempt at social revolution been successful. Political revolutions by coups de force have often been successful, but never a revolution in social relations. And yet, in spite of his own philosophy and the teachings of history, Marx was ready to believe in the Paris Commune of 1871, as the "critical event" which was to bring the Social Revolution to a glorious reality! There is hardly an instance in history of a more hopeless revolt. It was foredoomed to its tragic failure. Its hopes were not based upon reality but upon utopian romanticism. Yet Marx saw the suicidal revolt through the same rose-colored spectacles as the utopians he was wont to deride. He spoke of the insurrection as "a glorious deed for our party," and felt that it was to "serve as a lever" for the overthrow of capitalist class rule.

Just as he had done in 1848, Marx in 1871 succumbed to that exuberant optimism which is a characteristic of all utopian visionaries, and which he had rebuked a thousand times in others. As a theorist he had set forth in his conception of social evolution the futility of all attempts to change the social order by forcible means until the necessary economic conditions of its existence had developed. And yet, as a revolutionist, he forgot his own philosophy so far as to think that in France, where in 1871 petty production was still the rule, such a *coup de force* could succeed.

Now, it is only by citing such examples as these that the Syndicalists can make plausible their contention that their anti-parliamentarian methods are the methods of Marx. They must ignore the fact that Marx never refused to participate in parliamentary action, but, on the contrary, heartily approved of it, as witness the legislative programme in the *Communist Manifesto*, the legislative programme of the International and his approval of the German Social Democracy and its parliamentary methods. They must ignore, too, the numerous instances, to some of which I have referred, when Marx condemned all attempts by "militant minorities" to bring about forcible revolutions. To the Syndicalist this method which Marx satirized and despised is perhaps more important than anything else.

It is rather disingenuous to set up the plea that the refusal of the Socialist parties to join in attempts to change social conditions by violent means, to despise and discard parliamentary action and to adopt the methods of "direct action" by militant minorities, is the result of a corruption of Marxism by Engels or anybody else. The life of Marx proves the absurdity of such a view. Two years after the Paris Commune Marx and Engels in a new preface to the *Communist Manifesto*, wrote: "The Commune notably offers a proof that the working class cannot simply take possession of the State machinery and set it in motion for their own aims." What they meant is clear from the context. It was not, as our Anarchist and Syndicalist friends are fond of asserting, the hopelessness of parliamentary action, "possession of the State machinery," which they felt the

Commune to have demonstrated, but the hopelessness of the vision of sudden possession of that machinery and its immediate use to realize a great preconceived plan of social reorganization. What the Paris Commune really taught was that the proletarian revolution must needs be a long drawn-out struggle, the proletariat advancing slowly, step by step, but with great certainty, gaining courage and wisdom and experience with each advance.

When Engels, in 1895, wrote his Introduction to *The Class War in France* he reviewed this whole question. Referring to the illusions of an immediate triumph of the proletariat and the end of capitalism which Marx and himself entertained in 1848, he emphasizes the importance of the unripeness of the economic development of the time: "History proves that we were wrong—we and those who like us, in 1848, awaited the speedy success of the proletariat. It became perfectly clear that economic conditions all over the Continent were by no means as yet sufficiently matured for superseding the capitalist organization of production." Engels goes on to show that the economic expansion in Europe after 1848, including especially the rise of Germany as an industrial nation of the first rank, proves how far capitalism was at that time from the climax of its development, the point at which the integument of the old system is burst and a new system is born. That Marx would have subscribed to these words written by his great co-worker seems to me an obvious conclusion from his philosophy and his life as a whole: "The time for small minorities to place themselves at the head of the ignorant masses and resort to force in order to bring about revolutions, is gone. A complete change in the organization of society can be brought about only by the conscious cooperation of the masses; they must be alive to the aim in view; they must know what they want. The history of the last fifty years has taught that. But if the masses are to understand the line of action that is necessary, we must work hard and continuously to bring it home to them. That, indeed, is what we are now engaged upon, and our success is driving our opponents to despair."

Undoubtedly there are elements of Marxism in the Syndicalist amalgam, but the claim that Syndicalism is the pure gold of Marxism, unalloyed, is simply an example of brilliant literary daring— pure Syndicalist "nerve"!

III.

The Syndicalist conception of the class war is undoubtedly derived from the class struggle theory of Marx, but the two are not identical. To a very large extent in theory, and almost universally in practice, Syndicalists regard the class war as a huge *mélée*, a sort of Donnybrook Fair free-for-all fight, in which any act of workers which aims at the injury of capitalists, as such, is justified by its aim. That a particular act or series of acts directed against their employers by impassioned workers injures not alone the employers, but society itself, by retarding social development and destroying gains already made, matters nothing. Thus we find American Syndicalists saying:

> "The Syndicalist takes no cognizance of Society. He is interested only in the welfare of the working class and consistently defends it. He leaves the rag-tag mass of parasites that make up the non-working class part of Society to look after their own interests. It is immaterial to him what becomes of them so long as the working class advances. He is not afraid of 'turning the wheels of progress backward' in thus constantly confining himself to the interests of the working class, as he knows that by freeing the working class entirely he will give social development the greatest stimulus it has ever known."

In this declaration there is much that is, from a Socialist point of view, quite admirable and unobjectionable. But what of the avowed indifference to social interests, and the implied readiness to adopt methods to secure the immediate gain of the proletariat which are, from the point of view of society, retrogressive? The statement sounds suspiciously like the arguments offered in earlier generations to justify the destruction of machinery, by the Luddites, for example.

Even if the methods of fighting are such that their use involves deceit, treachery and cowardice, and thus tend to impair the morale of the workers, the Syndicalist concept of the class war does not lead to their condemnation. The typical Syndicalist boasts of this and scoffs at the "sentimentalism" of those who protest against methods which demoralize the workers themselves. He does not realize that the social revolution, if it is ever to succeed, will require moral stamina; that the attainment of a new and just social order is an aim which demands as a necessary condition for its realization the development in the proletariat of qualities the very opposite of deceit, treachery and cowardice. This is all the more remarkable by reason of the fact that all the shades of Syndicalist thought accept the view that the workers' unions are to be the units of social organization in the new society. There is something infinitely pathetic in this outburst by the American writers just quoted:

> "A few rebels can, undetected, saboge and demoralize an industry and force the weak or timid majority to share in its benefits. The Syndicalists are not concerned that the methods of sabotage may be 'underhanded' or 'unmanly.' They are very successful and that is all they ask of them. They scoff at the sentimental objection that sabotage destroys the worker's pride in his work. They prefer to be able to more successfully fight their oppressors, rather than to cater to any false sense of pride."

We shall presently have occasion to inquire whether the destruction of the worker's integrity as a worker is compatible with the Syndicalist aim. Here and now we must ask another question: What if the methods used destroy not merely "the worker's pride in his work," but his sense of honor, his frankness, his courage to avow his purpose, his faith in his fellows and in himself? That, it seems to me, is the real danger.

Can class solidarity flourish when the ways of class warfare are furtive, secret, subterranean? Or will these methods not make it easy for espionage and mutual suspicion and distrust to destroy the measure of class solidarity already attained? After the revolution of 1848, when the reaction set in, the movement of the time became a secret conspiratory movement. Intrigue within intrigue resulted, spies and informers were everywhere. Every man seemed to distrust every other man. The class solidarity which had existed was broken. Are not the furtive ways of Syndicalism likely to produce a similar result?

It is the essence of the class struggle theory of Marx that the social relations arising out of the methods of production take the form of class alignments, and that history is mainly the record of struggles between opposing classes. But progress is not the result of blind class rage. When a class which has been oppressed and exploited overthrows the yoke of the class to which it has been subjected, it does not destroy all that exists, but only that which limits its own freedom and development. It inherits much of value, alike to itself and to society as a whole. Each successive ruling class widens the area of freedom and adds to the sum of social well-being. Thus the capitalist system, as Marx has pointed out in the *Communist Manifesto*, has made numerous splendid contributions to human progress and the proletariat will inherit a great legacy of good to be preserved as well as evils to be destroyed. This heritage includes the degree of social consciousness already developed, and the socialized methods of dealing with the problems of society which have been developed in place of the barbaric methods of violence.

Of all this there is hardly a hint in the Syndicalist view of the class war. Indeed, in the statements quoted above, which are quite typical, there is a definite repudiation of much that is essential in our digest of the Marxian theory. I am compelled to class the Syndicalist conception of the class war with the numerous perversions of the Marxian theory which have obtained more or less vogue at certain times and places, a catalogue of which would make an interesting and curious addition to our literature.

For example, in Russia, in 1881, at the time of the Nihilist agitation by the Will of the People movement, a great outburst of anti-Semitism took place. Jews were beaten, robbed and murdered and Jewish women and girls were ravished and then tortured or murdered. Yet, on the flimsy excuse that many Jews were usurers, while the mobs who carried on the bloody work were mainly composed of Russian peasants, there were leaders of the revolutionary movement who saw in the pogrom a sign of awakening class consciousness among the Russian peasants. Even the leading revolutionary organ of the party was freely accused of giving countenance to this view. Incredible as it may seem, the Marxian theory of class struggles was put forward as a reason for welcoming anti-Semitism. "The riots show that the Russian people are capable of revolution," said these "Marxists" of the closet. "Let the people taste blood and experience the sense of power and then they will turn against their masters. This is no time to talk of 'right' and 'wrong.' What matters is that the workers are aroused. Their class consciousness is developing." Even Jewish Nihilists frequently accepted this view, despite the fact that the rich Jewish money-lenders were rarely molested.

It is well known that in France there existed during the 1880's a group of Anarchists who adopted a perversion of the class struggle theory and made the class war the basis of their propaganda. Their "revolutionary method" was to counterfeit money and forge cheques. By so doing, they said, they were helping to "demoralize capitalism," and "hitting the capitalist where he feels the blow most," that is, his pocketbook. In more recent years we have had in France garroting and highway robbery by the Apaches and organized robbery on a wholesale plan by Bonnot and his followers. The philosophy of these Anarchists was identical with that of the Syndicalists who declare it to be a revolutionary act to "demoralize an industry," and of those who preach to the workers the duty of "making the capitalist suffer," the only way to do which is "to strike him in the place where he carries his heart and his soul, his center of feeling— the pocketbook."

From the Socialist point of view, merely to "make the capitalist suffer," whether by hitting him in the pocketbook or inflicting personal injury upon him by violent assault, is not an act which benefits the workers. Therefore, such methods have no place in the organized class warfare. Only that injury to the employer which results in a corresponding gain to the wage-worker can have any justification. The worker for low wages who remains at work but, in order to "get even" with his employer, secretly wastes materials or spoils tools in order that the employer's profits may be reduced, does not himself gain by the policy which he pursues, nor does he advance the condition of his class. On the other hand, he usually does advance the interest of some other capitalist, his employer's rival. Unscrupulous capitalists have often been known to bribe workers employed by their rivals to practice sabotage in this fashion.

IV.

M. Lagardelle has published an interesting report of the conference held in Paris in April, 1907, by a number of prominent French and Italian Syndicalists to consider the broad subject of the relation of Syndicalism to Marxian Socialism. Perhaps the most important point made took the form of a claim to which most of the Syndicalists appear to have agreed, and which M. Lagardelle states in the following words: "If the whole of Socialism is comprised in the class war, we may say that the whole of Socialism is comprised in Syndicalism, because outside Syndicalism there is no class warfare."

Now, this is not mere bombast on the part of the brilliant French Syndicalist. Professor Lagardelle does not mean that there is no class warfare outside of that which we know as revolutionary Syndicalism; that there is no class war where the revolutionary Syndicalist movement does not exist. I take it that he means that outside of the fight waged by the labor unions, conservative and revolutionary, there is no organized proletarian warfare against the capitalist class. The struggle waged in parliaments, even by the Socialist parties, is not a class struggle according to M. Lagardelle. He denies that political parties express class interests.

> "Parliamentary Socialism, in its revolutionary, no less than in its reformist aspects, has lived upon the illusion that parties are the political expression of classes, and that classes find in Parliament a mechanical register of their respective forces. But experience has shown that parties, instead of being the counterpart of classes, are a heterogeneous mixture of elements borrowed from all social categories, and that there is no longer any real relation between the political influence of the Socialist parties and the real power of the working class. The truth is that Parliamentary Socialism has not only failed to open up any unbridgeable gulf between the proletariat and the bourgeoisie, but it has become one of the constituent factors of the State and one of the agents in the 'solidarist action' of the democracy."

There are two points which stand out in this very lucid statement challenging our special attention. The first is the peculiarly narrow limitation of the scope of class action. Parliamentary Socialism is indicted for its failure to "open up any unbridgeable gulf between the proletariat and the bourgeoisie" But why should it be? Why should that be regarded as the object of any proletarian movement, political or other? Surely, the "unbridgeable gulf" exists in the fundamental economic relationships of the two classes! It is not something to be created by struggle. On the contrary, the existence of the "unbridgeable gulf" is what gives birth to the struggle. It is the *raison d'étre* of political Socialism. That some reformist Socialists have seemed to attempt to bridge the gulf, or at least to deny that it is unbridgeable, might justify the criticism that they could not represent the proletariat. But to take the gulf and its unbridgeable nature for granted is surely not only compatible with the idea of class war, but inseparable from it, unless by "class war" we mean something other than the meaning which the term has borne since Marx's day. Taking the gulf and its unbridgeable span for granted, the Socialist parties aim, not to reconcile the proletariat to the bourgeoisie, but to wrest from the bourgeoisie measures which will strengthen the proletariat and better equip it for the struggle. The method may be indicted as inefficient—that is, however, beside the point we are now discussing. What concerns us is the fact that M. Lagardelle denies that it is a phase of class warfare, and that simply because it does not "open up any unbridgeable gulf between the proletariat and the bourgeoisie"— as superfluous a task, one would think, as could well be devised.

The second noteworthy point in M. Lagardelle's statement is the reference to the "heterogeneous mixture of elements" of which political parties, including the Socialist parties, are composed. It is true, of course, that no Socialist party is composed exclusively of proletarians. That is not a new or strikingly original discovery. Ever since the time of Marx it has been remarkable that so many leaders of the proletarian movement have come from the bourgeoisie. To name only a few: Marx, Engels, Lassalle, Liebknecht, Singer, Kautsky, Jaurés, Vandervelde, Pleckanoff and Hyndman have all been non-proletarians. But the presence of bourgeois elements is not a peculiarity of proletarian political parties. It is equally true of Anarchism, as witness Proudhon, Bakunin, Reclus and Kropotkin. It is equally true of Syndicalism, as witness Sorel, Lagardelle, Labriola, Leone, Berth, and many others. Indeed, the Syndicalist movement has from its inception been remarkable for the zeal with which it has been espoused by successful lawyers, college professors and journalists, whose "clean linen, good manners and elegant wives" have caused many to sneer at the whole Syndicalist propaganda as exotic. It is folly of the worst type to judge the spirit of a popular movement by these criteria. The proletarian character of Socialism or Syndicalism is not to be affirmed or denied by counting the noses of the non-proletarians engaged in its service. But M. Lagardelle chooses the test. Very well then, if the fact that Socialist parties contain a "heterogeneous mixture of elements borrowed from all social categories" proves that it is an illusion to regard those parties as proletarian, is it not equally an "illusion" to regard Syndicalism with its horde of intellectuals of bourgeois antecedents and training as a proletarian movement? And if not, why?

V.

This is not an argument based upon a single unfortunate expression by M. Lagardelle. The fact is that Syndicalist literature teems with attacks upon the middle class lawyers, professors, doctors and journalists who serve the Socialist movement, and upon the movement itself because of the presence in it of such bourgeois elements. Just as in the sixties of the last century a bitter anti-intellectualist propaganda was waged, especially against Marx and Engels, by men who were themselves lawyers, journalists and doctors, so today the same thing occurs in connection with the Syndicalist movement. There is the same flattering of the proletariat, the same attempt to undermine the faith of the workers in men who come to the movement from other classes. If this came from the workers themselves, inspired by a jealous fear for the safety of the movement, it would not be at all a bad thing. It would insure a watchfulness born of an active class consciousness. It is sinister because of its source. Whenever middle class intellectuals preach anti-intellectualism to the workers, one who is familiar with Socialist history instinctively scents schism and the conflict of personal ambitions.

That which determines the place of a movement or a party in the class conflict of modern society is not the exact status of the individuals belonging to it, but rather their consciousness, their view of life and the struggle, their aspiration. Unless we adopt this test, it seems to me, we are forced to the conclusion that the most corrupt political machines in our American cities reflect the interests of the proletariat, for the reason that their power is derived exclusively, or nearly so, from proletarian votes. They do not in fact reflect the interests of the proletariat because the proletarian voters who give them their strength have no class consciousness or aspiration. It is true, of course, that status and consciousness are not unrelated; that, as a general rule, the consciousness and aspiration of men is determined by their economic status, but it is not a rule to be strictly applied to the judgment of each man.

First of all, there is the great mass without any real consciousness or aspiration; the millions who are as unconscious as the driftwood which the waves cast upon the shore. Then of the conscious, those who realize that their material interests link them to one or other of the contending classes, there are, on each side, individuals whose acts do not conform to their class interests. There are proletarians who realize that their class is exploited and that only by union can it be emancipated, who, despite their consciousness, remain apart from their fellows, preferring the easier path of non-resistance to oppression, or of seeking to secure individual emancipation and elevation to the class above. On the other side there are members of the exploiting class who, fully aware of their class interests, prefer to ally themselves with the proletariat in the actual struggle. Often, as Marx observes, "they supply the proletariat with fresh elements of enlightenment and progress". But for such as Marx, Engels, Lassalle and others of their class, how would the workers have been roused to class consciousness at all? Class instinct they have always had, but the development of instinct to consciousness required education and mental training practically impossible for proletarians. Even the Syndicalist theories could not have been developed and popularized as they have been without the service of the gifted intellectuals who have devoted themselves to the task.

The Syndicalists can make a very plausible reply to this sort of *tu quoque* argument. The nature of their reply is obvious: Granted that middle class intellectuals may serve the proletarian movement loyally and well, they cannot lead it without undermining its revolutionary character as a class movement. Their leadership must destroy the class psychology of the movement. But the very nature of parliamentary methods leads inevitably to the selection of non-proletarians as representatives, as witness the number of journalists, lawyers, doctors and professors elected by the various Socialist parties of the world. On the other hand, the Syndicalist method of warfare, just because it is carried on by the workers, excludes this danger. As M. Leroy Beaulieu has remarked, in the *Bureau Confédéral* of the *Confédération Générale du Travail* "we can find no element of other than proletarian origin, not only the rank and file but the leaders are of popular origin and class, they either are or have been working men, they are neither *'literateurs'* nor of intellectual origin, nor have they the habits of the bourgeoisie?" This is very different from any of the Socialist parties, and the difference is inevitable. The bourgeois elements in the political parties have a peculiar aptitude for political life.

So much for the Syndicalist rejoinder to our criticism. In judging it we must bear in mind the peculiar conditions of political life in France and Italy. In both countries the way to political preferment has long been through the profession of radical ideas, and in both countries politics is a middle class profession. An Englishman or an American would hardly comprehend the French and Italian conceptions of political life. In Germany and in England the Socialist representatives in parliament are not generally of bourgeois origin. Of most of them it might be said in the words of M. Beaulieu's description of the French Syndicalists, they "are of popular origin and class, they either are or have been workingmen." Many of them are now classed as editors or *"literateurs,"* but they have attained that rank in the party service, frequently after entering parliament. Keir Hardie is an editor, an author and a lecturer now, but he was a miner. Bebel is an author, but he was a wood turner. In what way is Hardie, who was a miner and became an editor, lecturer and member of parliament, less of a proletarian than Tom Mann, who also is an editor and lecturer, but who failed to get elected to parliament? In what way does any Socialist workingman who becomes editor of a party paper and a lecturer come to be an intellectual, and another workingman who graduates to the position of editor of an I.W.W. paper and lectures for the movement remain a proletarian?

The fact is that, M. Sorel to the contrary notwithstanding, anti-intellectualism has no philosophical basis. It is a narrow prejudice, of Latin origin, developed among the most illiterate of European peoples, and has always been used by Anarchists to obstruct the political movement and by ambitious politicians seeking to control the movement.

VI.

Like the Marxian Socialists, the Syndicalists proclaim themselves to be revolutionists and avow that their aims can only be achieved by means of a social revolution. But their conception of the meaning of social revolution — as distinguished from the manner of its accomplishment — very materially differ. In so far as it can be said that there is a conception of social revolution peculiarly Marxian, it would be just to say that most Syndicalists reject the Marxian theory of social revolution. But there is little or no justification for the use of such a term.

It is true that in the preface to his *Critique of Political Economy* Marx defines social revolution as the slow or rapid transformation of the entire juridical and political superstructure of society, which proceeds from the transformation of its economic foundations. That, however, is not a conception originating with Marx. Moreover, the definition is not a complete description of the conception of social revolution which underlies all the work of Marx and the movement which has been so largely guided by his theories. All the non-conservative elements in society want social revolution in this broad sense. The Anarchist, the Syndicalist, the Socialist and the Reformer all want a social transformation. Yet the differences between them are wide and great. The Reformer, for example, would bring it about by fitting the juridical and political structure of society to the changing economic conditions in order to avert a clash of class interests. The Socialist, on the other hand, would attempt no such adjustment. He wants a social transformation which can only come from the clashing of class interests.

The distinction between the Reformer and the Socialist of the Marxian school is, therefore, a fundamental one. It is not a question of peaceful methods on the one hand and violent methods on the other hand. A mere reform may be accomplished by the most violent means, as, for example, the "bread tax" reforms in France in the latter part of the Eighteenth Century. On the other hand, a really revolutionary measure may be accomplished without violence. Such an event as the constitution of the French National Assembly, in 1789 about fifteen years after the "bread tax" revolts, which, accomplished without bloodshed, belongs to this class of revolutionary acts peacefully accomplished.

The essence of social revolution from the point of view of the Marxian Socialist lies in this: any act is to be counted revolutionary if it is the act of a class hitherto oppressed and exploited, through which that class gains additional power which it must use to transform the social structure in accordance with its own interests, no matter whether that transformation is gradual or sudden, slow or rapid. Thus, when Marx wrote in the *Communist Manifesto* that "the first step in the revolution by the working class, is to raise the proletariat to the position of the ruling class," and that "the proletariat will use its political supremacy to wrest, by degrees, all capital from the bourgeoisie, to centralize all instruments of production in the hands of the State, i.e., of the proletariat organized as the ruling class," he was not disavowing the idea of revolution. To wrest the capital from the bourgeoisie "by degrees" is quite as revolutionary as it would be to take it all by a single act.

Now, to the Syndicalist this is the rankest of heresies. He regards the Social Revolution just as the old pre-Marxian Socialists of the school of Blanqui did, as an episode, a cataclysmic event. He accepts the catastrophic theory that capitalism will fall with a crash and a new social order be raised in its stead. That Marx, contrary to the logic of his own profoundest thought, at times reverted to this view we have already observed. But the whole concept is utopian and anti-Marxian. It is, however, essential to Syndicalism. Without it the chief policies of the Syndicalist movement would have no theoretical basis at all. The principal revolutionary method of Syndicalism, the General Strike, which is offered as a substitute for the "antiquated parliamentary method" of class warfare, is to precipitate the great catastrophe. Otherwise it can have no sanction.

But the utopianism of Syndicalists differs from the utopianism of Socialists like Blanqui in one very important respect. The old school of utopians set out to capture society and its machinery. By conspiracy and insurrection they sought to capture the governmental powers, executive authority, and control of the armed forces. With these in their possession they might reasonably expect success. They could force the conquered minority into submission and give to their own acts the sanction of legality. The Paris Commune of 1871 shattered the remaining faith in that method. Our modern utopians, the Syndicalists, propose a very different method. Instead of capturing the authority of the State and its forces, they simply depend upon the cataclysm and chaos which the General Strike is to produce. They will bring things to a standstill, and then — well, they have a childlike faith that the State will be a hopeless wreck and that there will be no power anywhere, except the power of the strikers. Personally, should prefer to trust the way of Blanqui, to seize and use the executive power, rather than the way of MM. Sorel, Labriola and Lagardellel.

VII.

No statement of the philosophy of Syndicalism can satisfy friend or foe which does not take into account Sorel's theory of the "social myth." It is a rather subtle theory, not easily reduced to a satisfactory definition. It is quite impossible to believe that it is generally understood by the rank and file of the Syndicalist movement. Rather than inspiring the movement, it seems to me, it is a very clever and subtle thinker's attempt to interpret its psychology. As such it is of value. The best statement of the theory is to be found in Sorel's quite remarkable pamphlet, *La Décomposition du Marxisme*, though the subject is also treated in his larger works, *Les Illusions du Progrés* and *Reyfexions sur la Violence*.

Syndicalism has not yet developed a definite philosophy of its own. Its doctrines are not fully worked out. It draws freely from the Anarchist philosophy and the Socialist philosophy and contradictions are inevitable. Not merely do the different writers adopt contradictory positions which correspond roughly to their Anarchistic or Socialistic antecedents and affiliations, but the most careful and consistent of the Syndicalist leaders find themselves involved in contradictory positions. This is not said as a taunt or mocking criticism: it could not be otherwise with a movement so young and unformed. If Syndicalism becomes a permanent movement—as it well may—it will doubtless develop a definite philosophy of its own. Doubtless, too, the definition of its philosophy will have an important influence in modifying the policies of the movement. It will be necessary for the leaders of the movement to consider, for example whether sabotage is compatible with the basic philosophy of the movement and its goal. M. Sorel's writings are interesting mainly because they indicate that the development of this philosophy has already begun. I hazard the opinion that the Social Myth theory will permanently occupy a central place in the Syndicalist philosophy.

Sorel accepts the Marxian theory of the economic determination of social progress as a working hypothesis, but he combines with his materialist explanation the belief that ideas and the conflict of ideas constitute a much more important factor than Marx, or even Engels, who greatly broadened his view of historical materialism in his last years, ever dreamed of. He has a true Marxian scorn for the idealists and utopians who place dependence in ideas which ignore the fundamental economic conditions. He insists that the only ideas of value are those which are in accord with economic conditions and the trend of economic evolution. Such ideas, especially when they inspire masses, become great revolutionary forces.

Syndicalism is a religious movement, according to Sorel's view. Of course, he does not use the term "religious" in the conventional sense. Any great movement which inspires masses of people with the conception of a higher and better life, and so fills them with enthusiasm for it that they are willing to serve without hope of personal gain; to give their lives, if need be, in order that the great cause may be advanced, is essentially a religious movement. It is the same use of the word "religious" as that which has led to its application to Socialism, Anarchism, Trade Unionism, Antimilitarism, and numerous other movements. To a small movement Sorel would apparently deny the right to be considered as a religion, no matter how great the enthusiasm of its members, how noble their devotion to the aim of the movement. But if that aim is adopted by a large number of people, and becomes the inspiration of a mass, that fact makes the movement a religion.

The central impelling and inspiring conception of such movements is what M. Sorel terms the *mythos*. At the heart of every great social movement lies the social myth. At the beginning of his *Reflexions sur la Violence* Sorel prints a letter which he wrote in 1907 to M. Daniel Halevy, the well-known writer on French working class movements. In his letter Sorel sets forth his belief that the need of a great moral passion is the supreme need of the age. His own ambition has been to awaken in the hearts of as many men as possible the consciousness of a great vocation. He would inspire the individual and the class with a great vision. He believes that in every soul there is " a metaphysical-hearthplace." Somewhere the vision or, at least, the capacity for vision, lies and needs only to be awakened to consciousness.

Marx, according to Sorel, appealed to the proletariat by means of a social myth, the idea of a cataclysmic Social Revolution. Without reopening the discussion of the extent to which Marx accepted or rejected this cataclysmic theory, it is sufficient to get a concrete example of a social myth. We learn that by a "myth" Sorel does not mean a fable, or something which has been demonstrated to have had no real existence. It is rather an intellectual conception which cannot be either proved or disproved, which must be taken on faith because no amount of reasoning from experience can touch it. Just because it lies outside the appeal to reason it makes the stronger appeal to the imagination. Thus, so long as the Marxian conception of a social revolution is kept simple and men do not attempt to demonstrate it, but dogmatically assert it at all times, it acts as a great inspiring force. Men are lured on by the vision, the myth, of a great catastrophic event of immeasurable grandeur. That is why in earlier days, with its simpler and cruder conceptions of the Social Revolution the Marxian movement was so much more passionate and aggressive than it is today.

But the analysis of the myth is always fatal to it. Calm reasoning is destructive of the sublime imagination of religion. Analyze your myth and you become the victim of disillusionment.

"The myth is not suitable for division into successive slices of change which can be arranged in a series, and which, being spread over a long series of time, can be regarded as forming an evolution. This transformation is necessary in all action by a political party, and it has taken place wherever Socialists have entered into parliaments; it is impossible in the Marxian myth, which gives a revolution in a lump, like an indivisible whole."

Here we have the heart of the philosophy and the key to the Syndicalist movement. The myth, the inspiring idea, of the modern proletariat, was developed by Marx. It was the conception of the Social Revolution, a great catastrophic ending of capitalism and the realization of the New Jerusalem of its dreams by the proletariat. Marx gave a highly colored sketch, purposely free from detail. But now the myth has been destroyed, sacrificed to the necessities of the political struggle. The Social Revolution is now interpreted as a long drawn-out series of changes. It neither terrifies the master class nor quickens the heartbeats of the proletariat. It does not inspire the fanatical faith essential to revolutionary daring. There is no revolutionary ecstasy. The myth, of "revolution in a lump" must be restored.

This restoration Syndicalism accomplishes. It brings to the dying movement the quickening fire of the Marxian myth restored to its original state, "an indivisible whole." Only the name is different, the new name being made necessary by the presence of the corrupt conception which now bears the old name. The new name of the myth is the General Strike:

> "The Catastrophe —which was the great rock of oilense to the Socialists who wished to make Marxism agree with the practice of the politicians of democracy — corresponds exactly with the General Strike which for revolutionary Syndicalists represents the coming of the future world .... "

It is clear, then, that the theory of the social myth rejects the idea of "revolutionary evolution" which Marx held, and rests upon the old notion of a catastrophic social revolution. This social cataclysm is to take the form of the General Strike, when the proletariat paralyzes society by becoming motionless.

Syndicalism And The General Strike

I.

The term "General Strike" is used in so many different senses, to connote so many conceptions, that we must insist upon a definition of the term if we are to understand its use. If we are to take the term literally it means, in the language of a resolution adopted at the French Trade Union Congress in 1888, "the complete stoppage of all work." It means that the entire body of the world's workers will stop work and refuse again to labor until their demands are met. It means that every form of industrial activity is to cease. That men will neither produce food, carry mails, print papers, run trains, sweep streets, bury the dead, nor perform any other work until the master class concedes their demands.

If the term were always restricted in its use to this conception the discussion of the subject would be immensely simplified and clarified. Unfortunately, however, it is used to describe very different things. First of all, it is used to describe a strike which is general and widespread in a given locality. For example, if in any city a strike takes place and embraces most of the workers in that city, we speak of it as a "general" strike. The history of trade unionism is replete with examples of this sort of strike. Workers in a single factory have struck for better wages and have been joined by the workers in other industries. These sympathetic strikes have made what was the strike of a portion of the workers the strike of the whole body of workers or of a sufficient proportion of the whole to temporarily paralyze the community.

The term is also applied to a strike of the workers engaged in a particular industry when it applies to practically all the workers in it and not to a portion of them. Thus a strike of barbers in a single city would not be a "general" strike. If the strike should extend to all the barbers throughout the country it would be a "general" strike. Finally, the term is also used to describe a joint strike by the workers engaged in a number of related crafts, either nationally or locally. Thus, from time to time, the sailors and firemen have joined with the dockers, the coal porters, the stevedores and freight handlers in a common attempt to raise wages. Some such strikes have succeeded. They are commonly termed "general" strikes to distinguish them from sectional strikes.

Haywood, one of the most active advocates of the General Strike in the United States, says that there are three distinct "phases of a General Strike," namely:

A General Strike in an industry,

A General Strike in a community,

A General National Strike.

"There has been no time when there has been a general strike in this country," he declares. What he apparently means is that there has never been a strike in this country which absolutely stopped all labor in a particular industry or community or all the industries of the nation together. For certainly there have been local strikes of sufficient magnitude to be called "general," and strikes "general" in the sense that they affected whole industries. Further, Haywood declares that the conditions for any of the three forms of the General Strike have never existed. Apparently this applies to the world, not merely to America, for he proceeds to argue that, since it has never been tried, no one can say that the General Strike would not be a good thing: "The conditions for any of the three have never existed. So how anyone can take the position that a General Strike would not be effective and not a good thing for the working class is more than I can understand."

The naiveté of this argument is rather enhanced by the fact that Haywood refers with enthusiasm to various "general" strikes which have occurred, citing them as examples which prove the practicability of the General Strike. He speaks of "the greatest general strike known in modern history, the Paris Commune"; of the political strike in Russia he writes, "And coming down through the halls of time, the greatest strike is the general strike in Russia, when the workers compelled the government to establish a constitution, to give them a form of government"; he speaks of Sweden as "the scene of a great general strike"; of the French railway strike of 1910 as being "a general strike so far as the railroads were concerned" and "one splendid example of what the general strike can accomplish for the working class." He cites the railway strike in Italy as another example of the same kind.

It would be difficult to carry confusion of thought further than this. First we are told that the General Strike has been tried in many places, and are asked to admire and emulate the example set before us. Then we are assured that there never has been a General Strike, and that the conditions for it have never existed. We are asked to regard the insurrection of Paris in 1871, the rebellion of chauvinists dreaming of military honor and glory, of bourgeois republicans bent only on resisting monarchical designs, and of radicals and Socialists actuated by various motives, as a General Strike, "the greatest general strike known in modern history." We are also asked to regard the political mass strike in Russia as a General Strike, also the greatest in history!

II.

Now, when the Syndicalist advocates the General Strike he is not usually referring to the strike of workers in a given locality or industry for better wages or shorter hours. Nor of the political mass strike, the demonstration of their power by the working class by means of a strike in order to obtain some desired legislation, such as an eight-hour law or an extension of the franchise, or as a means of preventing war. It is not a weapon to be thus frequently used in the class war as Haywood and some of his followers seem to believe by advocating its use whenever labor leaders are in danger of imprisonment, for example.

No, it is something vastly more important than a method of warfare. The General Strike is the great final act by which the capitalist system is to be overthrown. It is to be the grand climax of all proletarian struggle, for which its strikes, whether large or small, local or national, are but the necessary preparation. What the Syndicalist has in mind is that the workers by becoming inactive, "motionless," destroy the entire structure of capitalism and create for themselves both the opportunity and the necessity for establishing a new social and industrial order. It is useless to discuss the General Strike at all if this is not understood.

The General Strike is to be the supreme act of the class war. It is the Social Revolution — "the General Strike is synonymous with Revolution," says the resolution adopted by the Congress of the *Confédération Générale du Travail* at Toulouse in 1897. Sorel accepts it as equivalent to Socialism and says, "The day is perhaps not so far distant when the best definition of Socialism will be 'General Strike.' "

It is important that this Syndicalist conception of the General Strike be borne in mind throughout our discussion. Many orthodox Marxian Socialists, like Kautsky, Adler and others, have advocated the General Strike as a method of working class warfare to be used under certain conditions. Among the advocates of the method are men distinguished by their unrelenting hostility to the Syndicalists, like Keir Hardie, who has advocated a General Strike as a means of averting European war, and J. Ramsay MacDonald, whose polemics against the Syndicalists have been vigorous and numerous. He declares: "I think that a General Strike — even an International General Strike—is quite possible for some definite and specific object which has stirred the popular mind, and is regarded sympathetically by sections of all classes— a General Strike, for instance, against an unpopular war." The most opportunistic of European Socialist parties, the Independent Labor Party of Great Britain, has, in the words of the party organ, the *Labour Leader*, pioneered the proposal that the workers should "lay down their tools when conflict is threatened." On the other hand, the intransigent British Socialist Party has scoffed at this as "a counsel of perfection," and declared that "a General Strike is never likely to be entered upon as a means of stopping a war, or preventing its outbreak."

It would be a grave mistake, therefore, to regard belief in the General Strike as the exclusive possession of the Syndicalist, or as the impassable barrier between him and the Marxist Socialist. There is no principle of Marxian Socialism which is incompatible with the belief that the strike, general or partial, may be used by the working class with great advantage, and prove to be a weapon of considerable, even primary, importance and value.

What is contrary to the fundamental teachings of Marx, and to the settled policies of the Socialist movement, is the Syndicalist view of the General Strike as a *tour de force*, sufficient in itself to destroy capitalism. The view of the General Strike as the Social Revolution, rather than as one of the forces bringing it about, is anti-Marxian. There is a world of difference between the two conceptions. To regard the General Strike as one of many methods which may be used to secure Socialism, is vastly different from regarding it as the only method to secure the triumph of Socialism.

III.

M. Mermeix, in his book, *Le Syndicalisme Contre le Socialisme,* ascribes to Mirabeau the credit of having first, in modern times, expressed the idea of a General Strike. Warning the ruling class of his day, the great leader of the French Revolution cried, "Take care! Do not irritate this people that produces everything, and that, to make itself formidable, has only to become motionless." M. Mermeix is not always reliable in such matters, and it is not unlikely that he has overlooked some earlier instances of the idea. It seems almost incredible that Mirabeau should have been the first man in modern times to conceive of the possibility of a General Strike. However that may be, there is no better or more forcible statement of the idea to be found in any of the numerous books and pamphlets on the subject. Labor needs but to fold its arms and become inactive in order to terrorize the world. In a single sentence we have a graphic portrayal of a world paralyzed, not by insurrection and bloody revolt, but by the non-action of the producing masses.

Ever since the rise of the modem trade union movement the idea of a General Strike has fascinated the minds of those engaged in fighting the battles of organized labor. The history of British trade unionism amply proves that the idea of a general stoppage of labor in all lines of industry has always been looked upon as a logical development of the partial and local stoppages affected by ordinary strikes. A strike is a stoppage of labor inspired by the thought that the employer will be compelled to grant certain demands to avoid his own ruin. If the public is inconvenienced by the strike, its interests will add another pressure to that already exerted upon the employer by the loss of business and its profits. It is easy to understand how the effective use of local strikes led to the belief that a strike extending to the entire industrial life of the nation would be quite invincible.

In England, from 1828 to 1835, the heyday of the Owenite propaganda, the idea of a General Strike was widely discussed and a few attempts were made to carry the idea into practice. From that time to the present it has been regarded as a logical development of the ordinary strike method, to be made possible by efficient organization. After 1835 little was heard of the agitation for a General Strike in trade union circles for some years. But in 1839 the Chartists, under Feargus O'Connor's leadership, adopted what was known as the "physical force policy," including the General Strike and insurrection. The Chartist convention of 1839 declared for the Sacred Month as a means of winning the political demands of the Charter. The "Sacred Month" was nothing but a General Strike. Immediately the movement had to face the stern realities of struggle against the powerful forces of the State. Insurrections and riots were brutally suppressed and by the end of 1840 nearly five hundred leaders were imprisoned or exiled. Desperate efforts were made in 1842, beginning with the miners' strikes in Staffordshire, to bring society to "the rigor of death" by a universal stoppage of labor, and again in 1849, the idea inspired the ill-fated demonstration on Kennington Common. That demonstration was to have been a dramatic warning to the English government, virtually a demonstration strike, but the force arrayed against it was too great. Six thousand armed police and eight thousand special constables with tens of thousands of soldiers secreted at strategic points and nine thousand openly displayed, was a force not to be overcome. The Chartist experiments with the physical force policy ended disastrously.

Interest in the General Strike died out altogether until the birth of the International Workingmen's Association in 1864.

That great movement awakened keen interest in every form of working class propaganda and struggle. Naturally, it led to a revival of interest in the General Strike as a means of class warfare. Up to 1867—the year in which the shoemakers of France formed the first organization which openly bore the name of *Syndicat*—the French workers had fought shy of strikes. Their experience with strikes, owing to the weakness of the unions, had been most disastrous and disheartening. But in 1868 there were many strikes. A regular strike epidemic swept over the country. The International was weak in France at the time, but the strikes gave it an opportunity to manifest its purpose and to win the support of the workers. The association raised funds in England and Germany for some of the strikers and thus secured the adherence of some large unions. The membership of the International in France took a big bound. By the end of 1869 it was claimed that there were fully 250,000 French members of the International.

But the increase of the numerical strength of the association was not the only result of the strike-movement. A more important result was the kindling of faith in the strike as a weapon of class warfare. France is not, as so many suppose, the classic land of labor strikes. That title belongs to England. The French leaders of the International had been rather opposed to the strike as a weapon until 1868-1869. Then, in consequence of the success achieved in a number of strikes, they changed their attitude and began to regard the strike as "the means *par excellence* for the organization of the revolutionary forces of labor." With the proverbial zeal of new converts, they began to instruct their English trade union brethren in the value of the strike as a working class weapon.

At this time interest in the General Strike was revived largely by the agitation of the French leaders, among whom Charles Longuet, the son-in-law of Marx, was most active. In Belgium it was advocated by that remarkable agitator, Caesar de Paepe. The thing was so beautifully simple in their minds, and so inspiring! On the other hand, the British trade union men regarded the General Strike as something remote. They had not forgotten the experiences of thirty years before and gave the agitation little support. But in 1868 at Brussels, and again at Basel in 1869, the subject was much discussed. In 1868-1869, the French leaders of the International, with the active support of Marx, Engels, and others, formed a federation of the unions of Paris, about seventy in number, whose objects as set forth in its "agreements" were very similar to those of the present revolutionary Syndicalist organization, the *Confédération Générale du Travail*. It was to "put into operation the means recognized as just by the workingmen of all trades for the purpose of making them the possessors of all the instruments of production." It was also to raise money to assist individuals and unions, and to assure to all the adhering unions on strike "the moral and material support of the other groups by means of loans at the risk of the loaning societies."

Not much was heard of the General Strike in France from 1871 to 1886. The Franco-Prussian War and the Paris Commune and their aftermath made it necessary to begin anew the task of labor organization. The idea was not lost sight of in the international movement, however. In 1873 a number of sections of the rival International, the Bakuninist organization, in Belgium and Spain passed resolutions advocating immediate preparation for a General Strike. At the Geneva Congress of the secessionists, in that same year, the subject was discussed at great length. There was a general unanimity of approval of the principle, but only a minority believed it possible to bring about an effective General Strike except after years of preparation. It was finally decided that a General Strike was not practicable at that time, but that the workers in the different countries should be urged to strengthen their organizations with a view to bringing about an international General Strike. Thus the question was "shelved" for the time being, but from that time onward the General Strike became a central feature of the Anarchist propaganda and programme.

The next great agitation for a General Strike broke out on American soil. In 1881 the Federation of Organized Trade and Labor Unions of the United States and Canada—now the American Federation of Labor—was formed at Pittsburg, Pa. In October, 1884, at the fourth annual convention of the federation, it was decided a to inaugurate a special propaganda in favor of an eight-hour workday. A manifesto was issued calling upon all the unions to demand the eight-hour day and setting a day for calling a nationwide strike in all industries to gain that end. The date first chosen was May 1st, 1885, but later it was decided to postpone the great event to the following year. The Anarchists took advantage of the agitation to carry on their propaganda, and on May 5, 1886, the Haymarket riots took place, with what tragic results we know only too well. Rudolph Schnaubelt's bomb — if it was indeed his—was perhaps the worst blow which the working class movement of America had sustained up to that time.

The tragic events of the American struggle created a world-wide interest. Sympathy with the victims of class hatred was widespread and the Anarchists of all countries renewed their agitation. In 1886 the first national federation of French trade unions was formed. It speedily became a mere adjunct to the political organization, the *Parti Ouvrier*, the Marxist party of which Jules Guesde was the leader. But in 1888, at the Congress of the Federation, held at Le Bouscat, the Guesdists were caught napping and Anarchists largely controlled the congress. At that congress a delegate and artisan, whose name was never recorded, it appears, introduced a resolution in favor of the General Strike which was carried amid enthusiasm, without discussion. The resolution read:

> "In view of the facts that the monopolization of the instruments of production and of capital in the hands of employers gives to the employers a power which diminishes proportionately that power which the partial strike placed in the hands of the workers: And that capital is useless unless it is put in circulation: And that the workers, therefore, by refusing to labor, destroy at one blow the power of their

masters: This Congress, recognizing that the partial strike can only be a means of agitation and organization, declares that the General Strike only, i.e., the complete stoppage of all work, or a revolution, can bring emancipation to the toilers."

The adoption of this resolution gave birth to a vigorous agitation for the General Strike. Foremost in the agitation, and the first to carry on a definite propaganda for the General Strike, was an Anarchist workman, a carpenter, named Tortelier. He was a man of fine gifts — eloquent, daring, tireless and honest. He drew to himself followers, some of them men of marked ability and acknowledged standing. Among these first place must be given to M. Aristide Briand, who later became Prime Minister and the man who crushed the great railroad strike in 1910. Briand has at times claimed the title of "Father of the General Strike," as, for example, at the Paris Congress of 1899, but that title is not really his. He was, however, one of the first to join in the agitation started by Tortelier, and boasted that he would be ready at any time to join the workers even if it were necessary to use "pikes, sabers, pistols and guns."

IV.

But it was not then the prevailing idea that the General Strike would involve the use of such violent methods. There was to be simply a cessation from work by peaceful and law-abiding citizens. The right to strike was guaranteed by the law, so that there was to be a peaceful social revolution by legal means. The General Strike was conceived as a very peaceful "strike of folded arms" — the *gréve des bras eroisés* — which would regenerate society. M. Mermeix describes this belief very aptly:

"The bourgeois who grows fat on the sweat of the people would waste away because the people would sweat for him no longer. The workers would carry out their strike with folded arms. They would not rush in tumultuous crowds into the streets. They would take a walk with their families, lunch near the fortifications, in the Bois de Vincennes, in the Bois de Boulogue, or even further out in those smiling suburbs where the rich capitalists, the exploiters of the poor, have their country houses. Would not this be a better way than that of the Socialist politicians, who advised the working class in the first place to vote for themselves, since their victory at an election must be the first stage towards the final victory; and who, once elected, would have no other thought except how to secure re-election?"

It was easy for Guesde and other Marxian Socialists to ridicule this naive hope of an idyllic passage from capitalism to a Socialist utopia, and they were unsparing. With merciless satire Guesde ridiculed the idea of a peaceful General Strike, and the belief that the master class could be so easily transformed into a part of the universal working class. The workers would be reduced first to starvation, for the bourgeoisie would quickly avail itself of all the existing food supplies. It would use the army to protect its interests and the workers would be "slaughtered like pheasants in a *battue*." When Briand made his great speech at the Congress of 1899 he held out the view that the army would be inadequate and powerless in the presence of a General Strike. It was suggested by one of the delegates that, in such a crisis, the government would possess a very simple remedy, namely the power to mobilize the mass of the workers, place them under military orders and treat those who refused to obey the orders as military defaulters liable to death sentence by court-martial. M. Briand airily dismissed this suggestion: "This would no doubt be possible, but I think the bourgeoisie would think twice before adopting it and placing rifles and ball cartridges in the hands of the strikers," he declared amid wild shouts of approval.

But in 1910 M. Aristide Briand, the former fire-eating advocate of the General Strike, had become Prime Minister of the Republic. When the great railway strike took place on October 12, 1910, the new Briand did not hesitate to do what the old Briand had so airily put aside in 1899 as improbable. The government issued its famous "mobilization decree," placing most of the railway workers under the immediate control of the War Minister as military servants. "Rifles and ball cartridges" were placed in their hands and the strike was effectually broken. On the 18th of October the Strike Committee issued its order for the return of the defeated strikers to their work.

Long before the great strike of 1910, the childish vision of a peaceful General Strike had been abandoned by all the Syndicalists save a few theorists and visionaries. The great majority of the active leaders preferred to look the facts in the face. They admitted the force of the contention of Guesde and other opponents of the General Strike, that the workers could not resort to that sort of action without inviting attack by the military forces of the bourgeoisie. Admission of this peril involved the necessity of attempting to weaken the military forces, hence the vigorous anti-militarist agitation which the Syndicalists have carried on. Every Syndicalist is an anti-militarist. To undermine the army is an imperative necessity. This fact is significant only as an evidence of the extent to which the ideal of a General Strike taking the form of a pleasant holiday has been abandoned. With the desire to destroy militarism no Socialist can quarrel. We may not agree to all the methods resorted to by the Syndicalists to accomplish that end, but with the end itself we are in full sympathy. But to the Syndicalist the military forces represent the power of the capitalist class organized as the State. Destruction of the military forces is simply a step toward the complete destruction of the State itself.

M. Sorel, it is true, has pictured the General Strike as a means for the possible accomplishment of the transition to the new social orders peacefully and without bloodshed. Apparently, he believes that in the numerous strikes which precede the great final event there will be developed, through violence, an irresistible passion on the part of the workers and a consciousness on the part of the master class of its utter powerlessness. At all events, against his hope of peaceful change must be set his apologia for violent methods in the present conflict. He argues that violent acts by the workers on the one hand and the employers on the other are not to be deplored. They serve to accentuate the class war. Workers who are filled with hatred for the capitalists to the point of fanaticism keep the revolutionary flame alive. The opposition to violent methods, which becomes increasingly characteristic of political Socialism as that movement gains strength and the responsibility of strength, is harmful in that it leads to a patient attitude, a calculating spirit, counting each victory and balancing it against each defeat. It is thus fatal to that sublime reckless daring and desperation which lead to heroic assaults on the existing order. He would admire Lassalle in 1862 contemplating a violent insurrection in Germany, rather than Marx opposing it as a mad and dangerous scheme doomed to defeat. He looks upon every manifestation of violence in the conflict between the capitalist and wage-working classes as a fresh evidence of the existence of a passionate hostility which will not be satisfied by any compromises; which will inevitably force the great decisive class struggle necessary to bring the new era to birth.

V.

It would be a grave mistake to regard this view of the role of violence, which might be called a psychological evaluation of violence, as a philosophical conceit peculiar to Sorel. The Syndicalist rank and file may not—almost certainly do not—appreciate the subtle reasoning of their philosopher. Sorel has not imposed a philosophy upon the movement: rather, he has given a philosophical interpretation of policies which the movement has from the first instinctively developed. The main policies of Syndicalism are based upon the necessity of keeping things in a state of constant agitation and turmoil as the means of developing revolutionary daring and passion.

That is why the Syndicalists are uniformly opposed to the policy of high membership dues, as distinguished from high initiation fees. They are equally opposed to both, but for very different reasons. They oppose, rightly, in my opinion, the high initiation fee because it makes it impossible for many workers to enter the unions. In some cases these fees have been raised so high as to effectually prohibit workers from joining the unions of their crafts. Fifty dollars, one hundred dollars and even, I believe, five hundred dollars, have been demanded as initiation fees by American labor unions! Some unions have closed their doors to all new applicants and with a "closed union" demanded also a "closed shop" Against such a stupid reactionary policy all right-thinking Socialists must protest. But the opposition to anything except small and almost nominal weekly or monthly membership fees is quite another matter. The union with low membership fees is always financially weak. It takes all the income to pay the running expenses of the union, no matter how rigid the economy practiced. Only the union with relatively high membership fees can accumulate big surplus funds out of which members can be maintained during a strike. In general, it has been the ambition of every union to have such surplus funds in order that at any time its members may go on strike with reasonable assurance of maintenance.

It would naturally be expected that a movement which depends almost entirely upon the strike, which utterly despises political action, would take this view of the matter which appears so practical and prudent. But it is the prudence which causes the Syndicalist to regard it with especial scorn. The rich union is rather apt to be very cautious, to be slow to strike. Employers, too, are generally unwilling to risk a strike with such unions as they believe to be well fortified and able to stand a long struggle without suffering. Unions whose members think it necessary to be "prepared for a strike," in a financial way, put off striking until they have accumulated funds. They do not always strike at the moment they feel the sense of outrage. They are cautious and prudent; they do not give free rein to their bitterness and act spontaneously. They want to assure themselves of success, or at least of the prospects of success.

All that is bad, a fatal defect, according to the Syndicalist. The union which is without funds, and which disregards all counsels of prudence, is best. It is "foot loose and free," ready to strike at any time, for it has nothing to lose. The absence of caution in the building of the organization will reflect itself in the recklessness with which the men will carry on the fight. So the typical Syndicalist policy demands low union fees, small treasuries, absence of calculation and preparation and a dependence upon the force of spontaneous enthusiasm and the sense of class solidarity. The maintenance of strikers must be taken care of by the rest of the working class. Appeals must be made to other working class organizations for food, clothing and money. Even the political organizations, like the Socialist Party, against which war is more or less openly waged, must be looked to for funds. It is a rather remarkable situation. The I.W.W., for example, permits none of its local organizations to contribute any part of its fund to the support of the political struggle. But whenever it has any battle to fight it expects the Socialist Party to provide it with a major portion of its funds. In the struggle of the Brotherhood of Timber Workers, in Louisiana, recently, the alliance of the employers with the State authorities was the central fact in the situation. Capture of the political power was the logical need. If the Socialists had appealed to the I.W.W. for funds to effect that purpose they would have been denied and confronted with the rule prohibiting such support. But the Socialists were expected to use their funds for the I.W.W., and did so!

The Syndicalist policy of intensifying the spirit of revolt leads naturally to the approval of strikes at all times. While the General Strike is regarded as the great final act of the class war, any strike is to be regarded with favor and supported. If it is merely a local strike, it will do something and there is always the chance that it may spread to other localities and give rise to widespread agitation and revolt. If it is a strike generally throughout an industry, it is so much more likely to produce a bitter feeling and, therefore, so much more desirable. If it results in violent outbreaks, the conflict with the authorities will tend to lessen respect for the State. Moreover, there is always the chance that such a struggle will precipitate the General Strike, the great ultimate and decisive revolution. This has led Jaurés, Pablo Iglesias, and others, to warn the workers that the Syndicalists, in constantly urging them to strike, are really playing a game of deception and trickery; that while urging strikes for the accomplishment of certain concrete ends, such as increasing wages or lessening hours, they are hoping and expecting that the workers will be insensibly and irresistibly drawn into a great comprehensive social revolution — the General Strike.

The attitude of the Syndicalist is easily understood. He believes in the General Strike which is properly described as the actual Social Revolution. He also believes in any strike which has not a political purpose, such as, for example, a strike to obtain the right of suffrage. A strike for better wages or shorter hours he favors because it will accustom the workers to that method of direct action and lessen their reliance on political action, and because it will serve to inflame their minds. A "demonstration strike," that is, a strike for the purpose of manifesting the strength of the workers and intimidating employers or authorities is approved for the same reason. An "irritation strike," that is, a strike which has for its object the annoyance and irritation of the employers or the public authorities has the same sanction.

VI.

It will be well perhaps to survey, briefly, the most important of the great "general" strikes of recent times. Most of these, as we shall see, have aimed at political ends, such as the attainment of constitutional government and universal suffrage.

In April, 1893, the Belgian workers declared a General Strike for the purpose of securing certain electoral reforms, especially a more democratic franchise and the abolition of certain property qualifications. A bill had been introduced into the Belgian Parliament granting universal suffrage and defeated in both houses. Then, on the advice of the Socialist leaders, a universal strike was declared for one day only. Some 200,000 workers responded to the strike call and in many cities industry was at a standstill. It had been the hope of the leaders that there would be no disorder, that it would be really a "strike of folded arms," but there were many clashes with the police at Brussels, Mons, Antwerp and elsewhere. Many men, women and children were shot down in the streets. But the demonstration was so far successful that in the course of a few days a new suffrage bill was introduced and passed, which, while it did not grant universal suffrage, did abolish some odious property qualifications and greatly extend popular suffrage. The elections which took place immediately afterward showed that the Socialists had a tremendous following. They polled 346,000 votes and elected twenty-nine members to Parliament. This so frightened the government that it hurriedly amended the new franchise law, raising the age qualification to thirty, and establishing a most iniquitous system of plural voting.

Now, in considering the Belgian experiment, there are several important things to note: The "strike" was short. It was really a demonstration of power. The workers did not attempt to measure their strength against that of the capitalist State. It was for an object with which a great part of the middle class fully sympathized as well as the working class as a whole, union or non-union, radical or conservative. The object, suffrage reform, was not one the attainment of which would have destroyed capitalism. As in the English struggle for popular suffrage, many members of the capitalist class joined in the demands of the workers.

In 1902 the Belgians tried once more to gain manhood suffrage by means of a universal strike. Out of some 800,000 workers about 300,000 went on strike. This time they were beaten, despite the fact that they once more had a large measure of middle class support. There were two reasons for the failure of this second experiment: first, and most important, the government was ready. It was not taken by surprise as it was on the first occasion; second, while as stated, the workers had a great deal of middle class sympathy and support, it was less general than in 1893 and there was more active opposition from that class. The strike failed and left the workers in a very depressed condition. It is the general observation of all students of the Belgian movement that the check suffered by the workers had a most disastrous effect, depressing the movement for a long period.

In Sweden in 1902, almost contemporaneously with the Belgian strike, the workers declared a General Strike in favor of universal suffrage. The conditions were similar to those which had prevailed in Belgium in 1893. The "strike" was essentially a demonstration on an imposing scale in favor of manhood suffrage. It took the government by surprise. The workers as a whole were united in the demand. They had the support of a large part of the middle class. In some cities there was a most effective stoppage of labor for a short time. In Stockholm, for instance, the factories were all closed, building was stopped, the public lighting system was completely stopped and all transport systems were rendered idle. The workers gained some concessions, just as their Belgian comrades had done in 1893, but they did not gain the end for which they struck.

In the following year, 1903, there was a General Strike in Holland for political purposes, but it failed as the Belgian effort of the previous year had done, and for very similar reasons. As in Belgium, the defeat of the workers had a very depressing effect and the movement suffered a very deplorable set-back. These defeats had the effect of checking for the time being the agitation of the General Strike as a panacea for the evils suffered by the proletariat. But in 1904 the developments in Russia revived interest in it. In October, 1904, the Russian workers rose suddenly, took the government by surprise, and by a General Strike of such proportions as had never before been known, forced the Tsar to grant, on October 30, a very ambiguous "constitution." That the success was not as great or real as was at first believed is now evident enough to everybody, but the effect at the time was to quicken interest in the method, to inspire belief in its superiority to parliamentary action. Since then the Russians have made two or three desperate attempts to repeat the strike of 1904, but each attempt has been a sorry failure. They have not been able to surprise the government and they have found that the great passion of 1904 cannot be rekindled at will. It seems to take at least a generation to fit the people of any nation for the great strain of a successful popular uprising. Those who shout for resort to general strikes upon the slightest provocation overlook one of the most plain lessons of history.

VII.

Passing over with mere mention of its occurrence the great popular political demonstration strike in Austria, in 1905, when more than 300,000 workers marched through the streets of Vienna in perfect order, forcing the assurance of a speedy grant of universal suffrage, which was attained, we come to the series of "general strikes" which took place in 1909 and 1910, in Sweden, France, Italy and Spain.

In the latter country the object was mainly anti-militaristic, directed especially against the sending of troops to Morocco. The movement was largely controlled by the Anarchists, though many of the Socialists were also concerned in it. The belief was that the popular sympathy was on their side, that the proposed expedition to Morocco was generally unpopular. Had this been the case, it is possible that the General Strike might have succeeded. It would appear, however, that the leaders of the movement were mistaken; that public sympathy was against them. The Spanish government was ready for the strike and crushed it with its customary ferocity. In all parts of Spain except Barcelona the movement was suppressed in a day or two. But in Barcelona the strike lasted six days. There was much bloodshed, the *London Times* giving the number of killed as one hundred and the number of those wounded as one thousand. Later official reports by the government put the number of those killed at eighty-six. When the workers from the provinces sent a deputation to Barcelona, 5,000 soldiers were sent out to meet it. The members of the deputation, who submitted to arrest without firing a shot, were cast into prison and then shot by order of a Court Martial.

The Spanish strike affords a telling illustration of the powerlessness of the workers to wage contest with the military forces of Capitalism. It lends great weight to the warnings of Bebel, Jaurés and other Socialist leaders. Says Jaurés: "If a general strike fails after it has changed into a revolution accompanied with violence, it will have armed it with an implacable fury. The fear of the governing classes, and even of a large proportion of the masses, will be given free course in a long succession of years of reaction. And the proletariat will for long years be disarmed, crushed down and fettered."

The universal strike against war is an alluring vision. To wage "war against war" by means of the General Strike is naturally an attractive idea to the working class. Probably it is the one purpose for which the method can be used with the greatest chance of success. But the war must be one into which the governing classes have gone against the wishes of the mass of the people. It must be an unpopular war if the General Strike is to succeed. But God pity the workers who attempt by a strike to put an end to a war, however cruel and unjust, which is not thus regarded by the vast majority of the people. It will not take the military forces to crush the strike: popular indignation will do that. Those of us who waged "war against war" in England when the Anglo-Boer War was on, learned to our bitter cost how vain it is to oppose the popular support of a war. There never was in modern times a war with less justification, nor one from which the aggressor nation had so little to gain. But those of us who waged the "Stop the War!" campaign took our lives into our hands whenever we spoke. And the risks and sacrifices were utterly hopeless and vain.

The general strikes in Italy, France and Sweden were quite unlike those we have hitherto discussed. They were primarily strikes for economic reasons, thus, the great Swedish strike was the outcome of a controversy over wages and hours. There had been a number of disputes over wages, local strikes of paper, pulp, textile and timber workers, and a general strike seemed imminent in 1908. When on August 4, 1909, some 200,000 workers went on strike it was their answer to a lockout of something like 80,000. The Italian agricultural strike of 1908 was, in the same way, an answer to a lockout declared by the employers. The French postal strike of 1909 and the railway strike of 1910 were due to economic reasons similar to those which generally produce strikes. The postal employees complained of improper treatment by officials, of humiliating rules and so on; the railway workers of irksome rules, low wages and long hours.

The French and Italian strikes were attended with a good deal of disorder and violence. In each case sabotage was practiced to a very considerable extent. In Italy the wounding of animals was a common occurrence, if reports are to be believed. The Italian strike ended in a miserable fizzle after lasting a month or more. The postal strike in France ended in a compromise, but with the supremacy of the government clearly asserted. The French railway strike ended in a most disastrous defeat. When the men went back they went back sullen and bitter to wage a campaign of sabotage. The great force of the State crushed the revolt. M. Briand became a great hero to the bourgeoisie.

The Swedish General Strike was very different. It was practically free from any violent manifestations on either side. From the very beginning the unions cooperated with the police in maintaining order in the streets. They were not attempting to paralyze society and to destroy the State. Their conflict was with the employers and their aim larger wages and shorter hours. The government remained neutral. It had done its best to avert the conflict by conciliation, but when the strike began, with full approval of employers and employees, it announced that it would keep absolutely neutral, interfering only to put an end to disorder. The unions, as stated, agreed to cooperate with the police in keeping order and did so. They suggested, too, the temporary prohibition of liquor selling as a precautionary measure. The result was a strike without disorder, a literal *greve des bras croisés.*

The strike committee at the outset disclaimed having any intention to overthrow the existing order, and announced that no attempt would be made to induce those workers to strike who were engaged in caring for the sick or for living animals, or those employed in the public services, such as lighting, the water supply or the sanitary system. They sought to inflict no serious or permanent injury upon society, but simply by means of a passive strike to so upset the routine of social life that the citizens would be stirred to active protest and interference and force the employers to concede the demands of the striking workers.

As a strike it was unusually effective. Beginning on the 4th of August with about 200,000 strikers, the strike grew until on August 10th the *London Times* sadly admitted that it was "an almost general strike." There was practically no disorder: the country was in fact unusually free from crime. There was no hostility on the part of the government, no use of the powerful repressive forces of the State, the police and the military, to crush the strike as there had been in other countries. Yet by the 16th of August it became clear that the strikers were to be hopelessly beaten. On that date the railwaymen decided by an overwhelming vote not to join the strike. On the same date it was reported that street traffic in Stockholm was being resumed. By the end of the month the strike was over, the workers, acknowledging their complete defeat.

VII.

What caused the strike to fail? It was not lack of organization, apparently, for no strike of equal dimensions was ever so well organized. It was not oppression by the capitalist State. The central fact is that, unlike the strike of 1902 for political reform, this was a strike by the proletariat for economic purposes. As such, it lacked the large sympathic support which had been accorded to the political strike of seven years before. Contrary to their expectations, the workers found that, after the first few days, they grew weaker each day, and that regardless of the fact that their ranks remained practically unbroken by desertion.

Time, instead of being on their side, was against the strikers. That part of the general body of strikers which was composed of men who had been rather indifferent and had struck with the rest rather than incur unpleasantness, grew sullen and restless. Then the great number of men who had become unemployed as a result of the strike, though not themselves strikers, grew more and more ready each day to take the places of the strikers. Finally, the small business men and capitalists discovered that they possessed powers which were quite sufficient to prevent the utter paralysis of society as a result of the proletariat becoming "motionless."

A great voluntary organization of latent and unused forces developed. In place of the usual methods of city transportation every automobile, cab, wagon or other vehicle appeared on the streets, ready for voluntary service. Coachmen in private service became temporarily volunteer public servants. Later, volunteers operated the street cars. Citizen volunteers cleaned the streets, wealthy men volunteered to deliver packages, to man ferry boats, and so on. Homemade bread took the place of the product of large bakeries. The social instinct of self-preservation was asserting itself. It was not inefficient, either:

"So efficient was this organization that a week after the strike began the streets presented very much their usual appearance, and the public suffered but little inconvenience from the social upheaval. It was something of an anomaly to see noblemen and officers of the highest rank driving cabs, merchants and stockbrokers doing ambulance work, civil engineers working in the stokehole of a steamer or attending to the gas, water and electric lighting machinery, civil servants acting as train conductors or unloading the ships bringing wood, coal and provisions to the capital. Yet all these services were efficiently and unobtrusively rendered, and it was clearly demonstrated that when threatened the upper and middle classes could rise to the occasion and do all that was necessary to keep the social machine at work and in perfect order. An attack had been made on the community but the community proved quite capable of defending itself. The weapon the strikers had most relied on not only failed to do harm, but had turned against themselves. The Public Security Brigade broke the General Strike."

At the end of August the correspondent of the *London Times* wrote of conditions in Stockholm:

"There are no outward signs of the calamity, though the sight of occasional groups of workingmen in their Sunday clothes might suggest that for some reason or other, work had been interrupted. Yet, as a matter of fact, the General Strike began on August 4th, and, apart from its paralyzing effect on industry, involved tramway and steamboat workers, cab-drivers, and the men at the gas and electrical works. How is it then that the trams are running, cabs are plying for hire in the streets, the steam ferries are working as usual, streets and houses are lighted, and there seems no lack of provision or of transport! The explanation is that these and many other of the most important social services are being performed by a brigade of volunteers, who have come forward in the public interest, and who devote their time and energies gratuitously to supplying the most pressing needs of society at large."

Two lessons, it seems to me, are clearly taught by the great Swedish experiment. The first is that no General Strike of sufficient magnitude to "place the country in the rigor of death" is possible except for some definite and specific object which has popular approval and has the sympathy and support of large sections of all classes, not merely of the proletariat. The second is that modern society cannot be placed in the rigor of death by the mere cessation from labor of the wage-earners. So long as there exists sufficient armed force to preserve the essentials of public order, the middle class in every country has sufficient skill and power to prevent the complete paralysis of society.

I know that some have suggested that this might be true enough of a country like Sweden, but quite impossible in countries like England and America. To me, that seems a very foolish and uncritical judgment. Nowhere are there better chances for the success of such a voluntary organization to defeat a General Strike than in the great industrial countries, England, America and Germany. Take the case here in the United States: What is our middle class? It consists of farmers, professional men and shopkeepers, for the most part. And who that knows anything of the facts can deny that an enormous number of these have had actual experience and technical training as manual workers? Among our farmers of the West and Middle West there is a surprisingly large number of men who have been railway workers, miners, mechanics and laborers, and they could, if they so desired, again take up the work they were accustomed to do and give a good account of themselves. Among our shopkeepers and small business men, likewise, the number of those who were formerly artisans is large. Many lawyers, doctors, preachers and bankers have worked at the bench and would not be utterly helpless if they were called upon in such a crisis to preserve the life of society.

Among the superintendents of industry are many who have risen from the ranks. The railroad magnate may still know how to run a locomotive. Our colleges, business houses and offices are full of men who have had technical training. Modern society is less helpless to defend itself against a "motionless" working class than any other form of society the world has ever known. If any "general" strike is to paralyze society it must take the form of a bloody revolution, a desperate assault, a matching of proletarian force against the force of organized society.

IX.

Now, what is the Socialist attitude toward the General Strike? The question is not so easy to answer as it appears. In the first place, no considerable number of Socialists anywhere believe in political action as the only effective method of proletarian warfare. In all countries the Socialists support the labor unions in their conflicts with the master class, and in general it may be said that the stronger the political Socialist movement is, the more importance it attaches to the struggle by the labor unions on the industrial field. Whenever a strike of any magnitude occurs in this country the Socialist Party invariably places at the disposal of the strikers its press, its organizers and other resources. The party machinery is used to raise funds for the strikers. Where the strike involves a clear issue between the workers and the employers, and is not due to strife between rival unions over questions of jurisdiction, the party gives all the moral and material support in its power, regardless of the political attitude of the unions or their leaders. It has supported the unions of the I.W.W. with as much loyalty as it has shown in supporting the unions affiliated to the American Federation of Labor. It raised more funds to help the strikers at Lawrence, despite the anti-political character of the I.W.W., than it raised for its own national political campaign fund in 1912. When the Garment Workers' Unions, affiliated with the A.F.L., went on strike the party at once placed its services at their disposal.

In thus acting the party has simply followed the established policy of the international Socialist movement. When, a few years ago, quarrymen in Belgium belonging to the "Catholic unions," which are bitterly anti-Socialist, were engaged in a great strike, the Socialists, through the party, the unions and the cooperative associations, went to the aid of the strikers with funds and supplies, enabling them to win their strike. The principle is the same as that which caused American Socialists to rally to the defense of the McNamaras, who were bitter anti-Socialists, Democrats and Catholics, as readily as they had rallied a few years before to the defense of Moyer and Haywood, who were Socialists.

The Socialist, then, is not opposed to strikes for economic gain, whether they are small and sectional, involving small bodies of workers, or big, widespread and general. On the contrary, support of such strikes is a settled principle of Socialist policy. Nor is the Socialist opposed to the use of the General Strike for specific purposes. Practically all the attempts to gain political ends by means of the General Strike have been initiated and led by Socialists. The Socialists of Belgium are at this moment preparing for another attempt to gain manhood suffrage by the use of this powerful weapon. At the time of the separation of Norway and Sweden, the Socialists of the latter country very plainly threatened the government that if any force was used against Norway they would at once inaugurate a General Strike to frustrate the efforts of the government.

At the Jena Congress of the Social Democratic Party of Germany in 1905 a resolution was adopted which declared that in the event of an attack upon the right of combination or popular suffrage the workers should resort to "the most comprehensive application of the general refusal to work." Among those who supported this declaration in favor of the General Strike was Bebel. Alike in the resolution and the speeches it was pointed out that the most thorough organization must precede any attempt to use this weapon. It was useless to depend upon the spontaneity of the movement:

> "But in order to render the use of this weapon possible, and as effective as possible, the greatest expansion of the political and trade union organization of the working class, and the incessant education and enlightenment of the masses, by the labor journals and by agitation and literature, is indispensably necessary.

> "This agitation must set forth the importance of, and necessity for, the political rights of the working class, especially for universal, equal, direct and secret suffrage and for complete freedom of combination; with references to the class character of the State and society, and the daily misuse of political power by the governing classes and authorities against the working class, in virtue of their monopoly of it."

Thus the greatest care was taken to present a view of the General Strike as a weapon vastly different from the view held by Anarchists and Syndicalists. In the first place, it is to be attempted only after the most careful preparation and organization. Secondly, it is to be used to gain or maintain political and legal powers and rights. Its purpose is not the supercession of political methods of class warfare but their improvement.

Despite this care, however, the adoption of the resolution caused great consternation, especially among the trade unions. Was the party going to adopt the Anarchist panacea, after all? Was it going to "play fast and loose" with the General Strike? Resolutions on the subject were passed in many places, the most important being that adopted by the Trade Union Congress at Cologne in the spring of 1906, which declared:

> "The Congress therefore considers that all attempts to set up a definite line of tactics by preaching the political General Strike should be repudiated; it recommends the organized workers to resist such attempts generally. The Congress

regards the General Strike, as it is represented by the Anarchists and people without any experience in the sphere of economic struggle, as beneath consideration; it warns the workers not to let the acceptance and circulation of such ideas distract them from the detailed daily work of strengthening their trade organization."

That is the great fear which has led the most active Socialists in the labor unions of the leading industrial countries to oppose the propaganda of Anarchists and Syndicalists in favor of the General Strike. They fear that reliance will be placed upon the spontaneous enthusiasm of the hour and not upon careful organization and preparation.

At the Party Congress of 1906, at Mannheim, the question again came up for discussion and Bebel delivered a notable speech on the subject in which he pointed out the great difficulty of instituting a General Strike against war. At this congress a resolution was adopted, confirming the resolution of the Jena congress, but declaring that it was not in conflict with the resolution of the Trade Union Congress at Cologne. The resolution is so important in that it states the relation of the party to the trade unions that it is worth quoting in full:

> "(1) The Congress confirms the resolution of the Jena Congress upon the political General Strike, and after declaring that the resolution of the trade union congress at Cologne does not contradict the Jena resolution, regards all disputes over the meaning of the Cologne resolution as settled.

> "The Congress again recommends specially urgent attention to the clauses calling for the strengthening and extension of the party organization, the circulation of the party literature, and the adherence of members of the party to trade unions and of trade unionists to the party organization.

> "As soon as the Party Council deems a political General Strike to be necessary, it must put itself in communication

with the General Committee of the trade unions, and take all requisite measures to carry out its course successfully.

"(2) The trade unions are indispensably necessary to uplift the class-position of the workers inside bourgeois society; they are not less necessary than the Social Democratic Party, which has to conduct in the political sphere the struggle to uplift the working class and to make its rights equal to those of the other classes in society, but which further, and beyond these immediate objects, strives for the emancipation of the working class from every oppression and exploitation, by abolishing the wage-system and organizing a system of production and exchange resting on the social equality of all— organizing, that is, the Socialist society: an aim for which the class-conscious workers of the trade unions must also necessarily strive. The two organizations are thus led to mutual agreement and cooperation in their struggles.

"To bring about harmonious procedure in affairs which concern the interests of the trade unions and the party equally, the central executives of the two organizations must endeavor to come to an understanding.

"But in order to secure that harmony of thought and action between the party and the trade unions, which is indispensably requisite for the victorious progress of the proletarian class struggle, it is absolutely necessary that the trade union movement should be dominated by the spirit of the Social Democracy., Therefore it is the duty of every party member to exert himself in that sense."

As Socialists we not only support all strikes for better conditions, and even advocate the General Strike for the attainment of specific ends, but we concede the possibility of the Social Revolution taking the form of a great universal strike at first and speedily becoming an insurrection. "I do not approve," says Victor Adler, "of giving our opponents the assurance, so soothing for them, that there will be no General Strike. That would be to encourage dangerous illusions. We do not wish to renounce the idea of the General Strike. But the question when, how and why it will break out, belongs to the domain of the future." And Kautsky says, "I am fully in accord with those words of Adler."

But, while the future may impose upon the proletariat the necessity of a General Strike, which must inevitably resolve itself into a great insurrection and conflict with the armed forces of Capitalism, and it would therefore be foolish to repudiate the idea as utterly impossible, no Socialist can regard the idea with anything but horror. If it ever becomes necessary it will be a great tragedy. Meanwhile, the mission of the Socialist movement, its *raison d'étre*, is to avert that tragedy. To be prepared to face the perils of insurrection if we fail to win by legal methods is one thing: to discard and despise legal methods and advocate insurrection is a very different thing. And that difference sharply divides the Socialist from the Syndicalist advocates of the General Strike.

The aim of the Socialist, as Wilhelm Liebknecht pointed out in a remarkable essay published after his death, must be "in the interests of a peaceful and harmonious evolution, to bring about the transition from legal injustice to legal justice with the greatest possible consideration for the individuals who are now privileged monopolists." That must be our aim, not because of any solicitude for the "privileged monopolists," but because the methods of peaceful evolution are of great importance to the proletariat, which aims to destroy nothing of value in the world it wishes to conquer and make its own.

Socialism must aim at securing a legal majority, at making the process of socialization legal and pacific. That is why we are a political party; why we seek to control the legislative, executive and juridical powers of the State. If we are swept by a cyclone of popular passion into a bloody struggle it will be because we have failed in our appeal to the masses, or because the capitalist class deliberately chooses violence. For the present and the immediate future those who, impatient at the delays of the political method, advocate the General Strike in place of parliamentary action, must be looked upon as more dangerous to the Socialist movement, and to the working class, than any of our capitalist opponents.

Sabotage As A Revolutionary Weapon

I.

At the National Convention of the Socialist Party held at Indianapolis in May, 1912, a clause was inserted in the party constitution, after a stormy debate, prohibiting members of the party, under pain of expulsion, from advocating "sabotage." Subsequently, the decision of the convention was upheld by an overwhelming majority of the party members voting in a national referendum vote. The clause reads:

> "Any member of the party who opposes political action or advocates crime, sabotage, or other methods of violence as a weapon of the working class to aid in its emancipation shall be expelled from membership in the party. Political action shall be construed to mean participation in elections for public office and practical legislative and administrative work along the lines of the Socialist Party platform."

The debate on the adoption of this rule was almost exclusively confined to the proposal to insert the word "sabotage," and for many weeks the party press was largely given up to furious controversy on the subject. It was the first time that the party had ever expressed any attitude toward sabotage; indeed, a careful study of the published reports of all the previous conventions and congresses of the party reveals no mention of the word prior to the convention of 1912. The adoption of the rule was an event in the conflict between two contending elements in the party—those who approved the traditional policies of the political Socialist movement favoring it, and those whose sympathies were more or less with the policies of the Syndicalists opposing it.

Few of the delegates who participated in the historic debate took the trouble to define sabotage in any way. To most of them the word was so new and strange that they found the greatest difficulty in pronouncing it, as one delegate who spoke in opposition to the adoption of the rule pointed out. Some pronounced it "sabbatige," others "sabbotaje," others "sabotayge" and still others "sabotaj." Only two of the delegates attempted a definition of the term at all. Both vigorously supported the adoption of the rule, and their definitions were necessarily partisan. Delegate Berlyn defined it as a violent method of dealing with the capitalists, literally kicking them out; "'Sabotage' comes from the French word 'sabot,' wooden shoe — putting the boots to them," he said. Delegate Slayton was more painstaking: "Sabotage as it prevails today means interfering with the machinery of production without going on strike. It means to strike but stay on the payroll. It means that instead the workers will stay at the machine and turn out poor work, slow down their work and in every other way that may be practicable interfere with the profits of the boss, and interfere to such an extent that the boss will have to come around and ask, 'What is wrong; what can I do to satisfy you people?'"

Now, the first of these definitions is as wide of the mark as anything could well be. Sabotage may be very bad and very dangerous, but it does not mean "putting the boots" to the capitalists. The second is much better, though, as we shall see, it does not meet all the requirements of an accurate and comprehensive description of the object of definition. Sabotage may be practiced in connection with a strike, by strikers, as well as by workers who "stay at the machines and turn out poor work." The word is used to designate many different kinds of actions, as we shall see.

But though there was little serious attempt to define sabotage, it was quite evident that the delegates who spoke on the subject had a fairly definite mental picture of the policy which is so designated. They might not be familiar with the French name, but like the Irishman who chanced an order of *pommes de terre*, they were familiar enough with the thing itself. It was not a new and unheard of method of fighting the capitalists which they were discussing, but one with which they had long been familiar under other names. In the words of John W. Slayton, they recognized it as "a line of action that is not new, although the term may be new in America."

American Socialists, like Americans in general, are little given to theoretical discussions and declarations upon abstract questions. If sabotage were simply a theory no rule against its advocacy could have been adopted. That a majority of the party members voting in the most discussed party referendum ever held, approved of such a drastic rule was due to a general recognition of the fact that Anarchistic and Syndicalistic elements within the party were carrying on a propaganda of anti-parliamentarism, sabotage and other forms of direct action, as opposed to the approved policies of the international Socialist movement. Like a parasite this propaganda seemed to fasten itself upon the movement. Its most active workers were holding places of power and importance in the party, and meetings arranged by the party at its expense for its political purposes were turned into campaign meetings for the anti-political propaganda by speakers who, paid by the party, scoffed at the futility of political methods.

This was abundantly shown at Indianapolis: "In the mountains of Pennsylvania have I met it," declared State Senator Gaylord of Wisconsin in a dramatic appeal for the adoption of the rule. "Out on the Coast, in halls hired by the Socialist Party for me to speak in, have I met it. All the way in between from the prairies of Texas far up into the factory districts of the cities have I met it." George H. Goebel, one of the party's ablest and most experienced organizers, gave similar testimony: "I speak again, as Comrade Gaylord spoke, from bitter experience. I have traveled in the service of this Socialist Party in practically every part of the United States, and what do I find? I find the movement in locality after locality disorganized .... Why? Because men have come into the Socialist Party and instead of advocating the principles and tactics of the Socialist political organization, they have advocated the tactics of an economic organization— sabotage .... If they are amongst those that want to talk sabotage, let them go out on another platform and talk it." Victor L. Berger declared: "Comrades, the trouble with our party is that we have men in our councils who claim to be in favor of political action when they are not. We have a number of men who use our political organization — our Socialist Party —as a cloak for what they call direct action, for I.W.W.ism, Sabotage and Syndicalism. It is Anarchism by a new name." John W. Slayton, speaking from a wide knowledge of the movement, said: "The fact is that these things [acts like those of the McNamaras] have been done in the industrial field, and the fact is that some men who advocate doing them come on our platform after we have billed the meeting and hired the hall and tell the people that they do not believe in political action."

Speaking for the Committee on Constitution, as its chairman, closing the debate, Morris Hillquit summed up the situation in these words: "Let us be frank with each other on the subject. If there had not been any Socialists advocating these measures we would not be discussing it [the rule] here now. Is it a pure accident that all those comrades who think the word 'sabotage' irrelevant happen to be the same who may perhaps be suspected of a fondness for these matters? I know personally of instances where prominent members of the party on public platforms did advocate just these things. Every one of you know. Why hide from it? I fear that our self-styled revolutionary comrades haven't always got the courage of their convictions. Why, comrades, if this is so absolutely improper for a Socialist constitution, why don't you simply vote against it? Why do you want to strike out the section entirely? Why don't you put it to the test? Why don't you stand up for it?"

We know now why the Socialist Party of the United States in 1912 made the advocacy of sabotage, crime or violence a bar to membership in the party. It was an act of self-preservation. It had been supposed that the exclusion of the Anarchists by the International Socialist Congress in 1896, in London, had once and for all settled the point at issue between the advocates of political action and the advocates of direct action. But the Syndicalist movement in various countries has brought the old Anarchistic teachings and methods of warfare into the party by a side door, as it were. Hillquit admirably expressed the fear of the majority of the party:

> "It has taken this movement about thirty-five years to come to the point where we are beginning at last to see the fruit of a generation's work, and I say, if there is one thing in this country that can now check or disrupt the Socialist movement, it is not the capitalist class, it is not the Catholic Church; it is our own injudicious friends from within."

How far the rule will accomplish the purpose for which it was devised remains to be seen. That will be the real test of the party temper. There are bound to be many opportunities for testing the real feeling of the party on the subject. For example, on December 14, 1912, *Social Justice*, a Socialist paper published at Pittsburg, edited by a Socialist who in the elections of the previous month had been the candidate of his party for Congress, contained on the front page an article calling upon the steel mill workers to practice sabotage. In heavy black type the article is captioned. "Arouse, Slaves, and Practice Sabotage." Because a timetaker in the Homestead Steel Works had been discharged for taking part in a parade of the striking trainmen at Homestead, the paper called upon all the workers to practice sabotage: "Spoil their products as the railroad boys did the night they struck and left the hot metal cool without hauling it. Let us rise in our might and employ the weapon they fear most, the weapon that struck terror to the Woolen Trust Barons. Let us employ Sabotage in the plants, organize industrial unions, prepared for a great general strike; Let us begin to teach Sabotage openly to the working class—On with the battle — War to the knife —Sabotage! General Strike! Eight-Hour Day! Minimum Wage! One Big Union!"

II.

The word "sabotage" was first used, I believe, in 1897 in a report to the Congress of the *Confédération Générale du Travail,* which met that year at Toulouse. Among the reports considered by the congress was one dealing with the use of the boycott and the policy which had been adopted by the British unions of workers engaged in the trades connected with the ocean transport services, popularly known as Ca'Canny. This report was written by Emile Pouget and Paul Delassale, both well-known Anarchists. They wanted to find a French equivalent for the Scotch colloquialism, Ca'Canny, as the purpose of their report to the congress was to elaborate the British policy known by that name and recommend it to the French unions. They "coined" the word sabotage. Never before had it been used.

To understand the meaning of sabotage, then, we cannot do better than begin with Ca'Canny, the British policy, and then trace its development when transplanted to French soil. And here I must become personal, reminiscent, autobiographical. I cannot tell the story of Ca'Canny from books—so far as I know it has not been authoritatively written. But it happens that I was actively and intimately identified with its earliest presentation and must share with others the responsibility for it. The autobiographical note which would otherwise be unpardonable seems, therefore, inevitable.

The period of 1895-1897 witnessed a revival of interest in the idea of industrial unionism on the part of many British trade unions. Schemes for the federation of trade unions were numerous. The idea was "in the air." Local Central Trades and Labor Councils were formed and a national federation of these attempted. Of one of these councils, in an important seaport town, as a working granite cutter, I was for years a member and for two or three years president and chairman of the Executive Committee. I was active, also, in the movement to federate the councils into one great national body, lecturing on the subject and doing a good deal of pioneer organizing. Like most of the young men of the time, I was literally inspired by what was, to me, the new conception of trade unionism. From one end of England to the other I preached the ideal of "One Big Union." No religious zealots ever devoted themselves with more faith and energy to a thankless task than did the small band of men with which I was identified. At one time I was president of the Trades and Labor Council; chairman of its Executive Committee; member of the National Executive Committee of the Social Democratic Federation; Secretary of the local branch of the Dockers' Union; organizer for the Seamen's and Firemen's Union in the district; and editor of a local weekly paper. In addition to these activities I worked at my trade, lectured for the Socialist movement and was active in my own union. And through all the feverish activity vibrated the passion for the "new" industrial unionism.

When the Seamen's and Firemen's union, the Dockers' Union and various unions of longshoremen, coal trimmers and other workers employed in connection with ocean and river transportation formed the International Federation of Ship, Dock and Riverside Workers, I threw myself into the work of organization. The federation was an aggressive movement on the lines of industrial organization. Its scope was international.

"The capitalist crocodile snaps its jaws in Hamburg when you step on its tail in London, Liverpool or New York," we said, "therefore we must organize so that when our brothers strike in Hamburg or Rotterdam or New York, we can strike at all other great ports in the world." Men like Joseph Havelock Wilson, M.P., Leslie M. Johnson, Tom Mann, Tom McCarthy, Edward McHugh, Ben Tillet, Charles Lindley of Stockholm, and many others, preached the new gospel with a zeal never excelled. Our hopes were keyed to a high pitch. The governments of the Continent were alarmed, and our organizers who were sent to Continental ports to organize the British sailors or firemen were arrested and ordered to leave.

A series of important strikes in the leading British and Continental seaports were lost, however, despite all the efforts we made. We were ignominiously beaten again and again. Then it was that the problem of what to do to hold together the magnificent organization we had developed presented itself. We could not sit and watch it fall to pieces. A new inspiration was needed; a policy to kindle enthusiasm, with popular watchwords and battle cries. The agitation must be maintained with even greater vigor than before, and for that some policy which could be crystallized into a phrase was needed.

For the moment it was idle to talk of strikes. Men were sick to death of strikes which always ended in their defeat. Political action, the election of workingmen to Parliament, was discussed, but that seemed quite hopeless. The British Labor Party had not yet been born. The Social Democratic Federation had not elected a single member to the House of Commons. Keir Hardie, the only Socialist ever elected to sit in that body — if we exclude John Burns, who had left the Social Democratic Federation, and was already dreaming of a Cabinet portfolio in a Liberal Ministry —was no longer a member, having been defeated for reelection at South West Ham. True, there were several "Labor M.P.'s" of the Broadhurst and Fenwick type — but they were simple Liberals who happened also to be union officials of the conservative school. Even Havelock Wilson, of our own group, was a Liberal and sat as one, holding his position by grace of the Liberal Party, which was financed largely by the very shipowners we were fighting! Upon all questions affecting seamen and dock laborers Wilson was splendidly aggressive and independent in the House of Commons, but otherwise he was a typical Liberal.

Moreover, the appeal for political action was all the more hopeless to our minds because so large a percentage of the men we were trying to organize had no votes. The proletarian of the sea is rarely a voter and among the workers employed on the docks and wharves there is always a large percentage of non-voters. They lack permanent abodes and independent homes entitling them to the franchise. With the strike discredited for the time being, and no hope of success in political action, the outlook was cheerless indeed. Then it was that, largely as a result of Leslie Johnson's inspiration, the policy of Ca'Canny was decided upon.

The old Scotch colloquialism was chosen as a picturesque expression of the idea of striking by stealth while keeping on the pay roll. The phrase means "go slow" or "be careful not to do too much." It is the equivalent of the English slang use of the word "soldier." When a workingman takes every advantage to slacken his efforts and to waste his time he is said by the English to be "soldiering." This, then, was the central idea of our Ca'Canny policy. We urged the workers to regard the employer and his agents as their natural enemies, and to regard it as their duty to their class to "strike the employers' pocketbooks, their real souls" in every way possible. A familiar story told was of some Chinese coolies who, when refused an increase of wages, promptly cut off a large part of their spades, saying, "small pay, small work." The workers were urged to obstruct the machinery of production wherever possible, having regard only to the safety of human lives. The laborer must take fewer barrow trips and take less in each load.

Of course this idea was very easily extended. From the slowing up of the human worker to the slowing up of the iron worker, the machine, was an easy transition. A little dust in the bearings, especially emery dust, would do much. Soap in boilers would retard the development of steam. Judiciously planned "accidents" might easily create confusion for which no one could be blamed. A few "mistakes" in handling cargoes might easily cost the employers far more than a small increase of wages would. "Keep this up," we said, "and in a little while the employers will be on their knees to the union, begging us to restore our efficiency as workers." Such, then, was Ca'Canny. It was a policy born of reckless despair.

At the Indianapolis convention, only one delegate among those who discussed sabotage and other forms of direct action attributed them to despair. Job Harriman, of Los Angeles, said:

> "There are some within the political party that are losing hope in political action .... On the other hand, the labor movement having conducted its fights on the line of strikes and boycotts alone . . . there are men there who, having come up against the trusts, have lost hope in the efficacy of the strike and the boycott. Thus standing separately, and having lost hope, they tend toward direct action of Syndicalism. Whenever a nation loses hope of a peaceful solution of a problem, that moment all the elements of war are present. Whenever a class or a portion of a class loses hope in its policies, loses confidence in its policy, all the elements of war are there and the idea of direct action grows and a change takes place."

And again, attributing sabotage to the separation of the political organization and the labor unions:

> "It is caused by the separation of the two great movements of America. They are weak and the weakness begets a hopelessness, and the hopelessness begets the fight. There you are. Every blessed man who doesn't want this 'sabotage' in our platform or in our constitution comes in — not every one of them but many of them —comes into our party and teaches it on the platform.

"Now, listen, boys. You cannot find a trade union constitution in America that puts it in there. Why? They don't dare to put their sabotage in, but you propagate it upon our platform, you commit the great Socialist Party to it, and we must defend ourselves against it, because, between the two great movements is being born today the Syndicalist movement. I tell you the heart and the soul and the blood of the Syndicalist movement is sabotage. There isn't a man that believes in it that dares to stand up and say 'I did it.' Of course not. I know what the conditions are; I know that the men oft-times have to fight for their lives, and when the struggle is on there is no telling what will be done; but we must say, we cannot teach it nor countenance it. If you do, and you permit it to absorb you, it will dissolve you and destroy you. Just look at it for a moment, look at what you are up against. On top of it comes the detective, back of it the police, back of it the judge to construe the law; all the evidence would be against us. You are expecting us to stand for a thing that not only will dissolve us, but that will put all the weapons in the hands of the other man. Why is it, men, that the great German movement has practically no Syndicalism? Why is it? One of my friends here last night laughed and said it was because they were of the Teutonic race, and the other fellow was of the Italian race. Partly, yes, but not all. Whenever you are separated, whenever you are. weak, any weapon is the weapon of the man in despair, and this is the weapon of the boys that have lost hope in political action and are losing hope .... They have lost their hope and the birth of Syndicalism is right here in our convention if we do not understand the facts."

In view of the experience gained in Great Britain, knowing well the forces which led to the adoption of the Ca'Canny policy, I am satisfied that Job Harriman rightly attributed belief in sabotage to lack of faith in the strike on the one hand and political action on the other hand. It is the policy of desperate and despairing men.

III.

The new policy, for a time at least, struck terror into the hearts of the employing class of England. That they soon found a way to meet it we shall presently see, but for a time they were genuinely frightened. They could not tell how to cope with a policy so furtive and difficult of detection. It was quite natural, therefore, that Anarchists like MM. Pouget and Delassale should be attracted to it. That it depended upon individual acts, furtively performed, was a distinct charm to them. They knew, of course, that it has been the universal habit of oppressed or discontented workers to deliberately lessen the quantity and quality of their work, on the principle of "poor work for poor pay." It is, in fact, the most primitive of all forms of retaliation by oppressed classes. That fact was another great merit of the policy in their opinion. A practice which so corresponded with an almost universal instinct of the oppressed workers would be easily understood and generally accepted.

In France, especially in the rural districts, it has long been the custom to liken the slow and clumsy worker to one wearing wooden shoes, called "*sabots.*" The phrase, *travailler a coups de sabots*, to work as one wearing wooden shoes, has long been used with reference to the slow and clumsy worker, the "old soldier" as they say in England. It is so used, I think, by Balzac. The idea is obvious: the peasant with heavy wooden shoes walks clumsily and slowly in comparison with those who wear shoes of leather. So the word "*sabotage*" — literally "wooden shoeage" — was coined by Pouget and by him and Delassale used in their report to the Toulouse Congress of the *Confederation Generate du Travail* as a good translation of the British term Ca'Canny. So much for the history of the word and its etymology.

Now, what was to the British worker a very simple matter of fact became the basis of an elaborate French theory. The British mind is not given to political and social theorizing. We saw only the fact that we could inflict injury upon the employers, and so force them to deal with the unions and grant the workers' demands. We had no theories; we did not need them. But when our policy was transplanted to French soil it immediately became the subject of theorizing. Men wrote articles and pamphlets justifying it and attributing to it all sorts of virtues and philosophical sanctions of which we had never dreamed. Sabotage was taken into the political laboratory, so to speak, and carefully dissected, its different parts being precisely described and labeled.

There has been developed a technology of sabotage. For example, the barbers of Paris, failing to obtain the better wages they demanded by striking, went back to work and resorted to sabotage. At night or in the very early morning hours they would throw potassium against the painted shop fronts, hideously staining them, so that the proprietors would be under the necessity of having them repainted. This they would do again and again. No sooner would a shop front be repainted than the vandalism would be repeated. It is said that of something over 2,200 barber shops in Paris more than 2,000 were so treated between 1902 and 1906. The employers were glad in most cases to make terms with their employees after two or three such costly experiences. Hence it was regarded as a very successful method and an important form of sabotage. So in the literature on the subject "*badigeonage*" occupies a very important place.

Of course, there is nothing new in such spiteful defacement of property. Petty quarrels between individuals, political fights and strikes, have often enough led to window smashing, splashing newly painted buildings with paint or tar or mud, and similar outrages. What might be regarded as original, or at least unusual, was the systematic use of the method by the workers as a means of extorting from their employers the increase of wages they demanded. Of course, also, the method opened the way for all sorts of blackmailing acts by individuals. It is obvious enough that unscrupulous persons could easily make use of a campaign of the sort to further their own interests. It was a form of sabotage which we had never advocated in our Ca'Canny propaganda in England, though it was a logical development of the idea of hitting the enemy in the pocket.

Another form of sabotage developed in France was called *la bouche ouverie*, or "the open mouth." The form is especially adapted for the use of shop clerks, waiters, and others who come into direct contact with the customers of the business man against whom it is directed. For example, a drug clerk receives a prescription to be filled: Taking advantage of the absence of his employer or superintendent, he whispers to the customer that the prescription calls for one or two simple drugs which can be purchased for one-twentieth of the amount which will be charged for the filling of the prescription in the usual way. The customer takes the hint and the proprietor of the business is "hit in the pocket." The clerk in the grocery store exposes the worthlessness of his employer's merchandise and causes the customer to go elsewhere. The waiter secretly whispers to the customer that the conditions in the kitchen are bad, that the cook has a skin disease, and so on, causing the customer to leave and so hurting the business of the establishment. The method is susceptible of an infinite variety of applications. It can also be easily abused, for a lie may be told as readily as the truth, if necessary. It may not be true that the cook has a skin disease, but what matters it if the customer is sickened?

The "open mouth" principle, that is, the revelation of disagreeable facts about a business, may be practiced on a larger scale, collectively, by the publication of the facts. Libel laws may be evaded by resorting to handbills distributed over a wide area. Those who remember the disagreeable revelations concerning conditions in the Chicago packing houses will be able to understand how the workers themselves might have exposed the use of bad and diseased meat, and so caused people to abstain from the sausage, potted meat and meat extracts. Or, they might have threatened the public and scared them by the publication of their intention to spoil the food products unless their demands were granted. Such a notice would undoubtedly frighten a great many people into abstinence from meat, as the revelations of conditions in Chicago proved. The butcher workmen of Vienna are said to have successfully adopted this method. The public got its notice and after that whole rat legs and other easily identifiable portions of the bodies of rodents in the breakfast sausage led to a big falling off of the demand for that particular article.

Candy makers could easily "warn" the public and then proceed to let chunks of terra alba, the white clay largely used in the manufacture of some of the cheaper grades of candy, get into the candy in lumps which could not be overlooked. Bakers and confectioners could first warn the customers of their employers and then use enough bad eggs to discredit the cakes and pies and injure their employers' business. The possibilities of this method of assault upon the profits of business are almost incalculable. Even if the workers stick rigidly to the facts, there is so much adulteration of food products, so general a use of bad and deleterious materials, that exposure must hurt the profits of the manufacturers.

But the employer who is not guilty, whose merchandise is really free from the evils of adulteration and the use of bad materials, is not immune. The workers are in a position to discredit his wares if they will. They can bring in the impure and foreign substances and secretly use them. I have heard a baker boast of having caught roaches at home and placed them in the bread. Moreover, as in every other form of sabotage, the way is open for one employer or set of employers to corrupt the workers of rival employers, and bribe them to ruin successful competitors. Just as labor leaders have been induced by one set of employers to cause strikes to be brought against another set of employers, so sabotage can be used. Only it is far more easily done than in the case of the strike. The whole union need not be misled. Sabotage is an individual weapon and can be practiced by one or two individuals unknown to their fellow workmen.

There are many other forms of sabotage, not all of which have been definitely named. There is first of all the "strike of the machine." When men are out on strike and losing, their places being taken by strikebreakers, a few of the strikers profess penitence and go back to work for the purpose of disabling machinery. In other cases, they take time by the forelock and disable the machinery before leaving. It is easy to break, hide or take away some indispensable part of a complicated machine not easily replaceable. Thus, in a strike of railwaymen or telegraphers, telegraph and signal wires are cut, cement is placed in switches, engines are run into turntable pits, and so on.

Again, there is the *greve perlée*, the pearled strike, or strike of passive resistance in which the workers simply stay at work but do their best to create confusion and loss by making "mistakes" and in general becoming as inefficient as possible. Clerks in a department store make the most exasperating "mistakes": a prim, elderly maiden lady receives a complete infant's wardrobe, or a crusty old bachelor receives the lingerie of a young lady who in turn receives the pyjamas intended for the bachelor. In the case of the *greve perlée* practiced in France by the railroad workers in 1910, after the defeat of their great strike, the confusion caused was enormous. Some of the strikers had been victimized and "blacklisted," and, in revenge, their comrades so mixed up freight orders that the greatest confusion resulted. There were at one time thousands of car loads of "lost" freight in the railway sidings — most of them containing perishable products, such as milk, fish, fruit and vegetables.

Still another form of sabotage practiced by shop clerks and waiters consists of charging the customer too little for the goods purchased. High-priced articles are wrapped up instead of the cheaper ones really purchased. Drug clerks charge ridiculously small prices for the most costly prescriptions. Waiters in making up the dinner checks "forget" to include expensive items, and so on. Generally, of course, the customer does not complain. If he does, the "mistake" is set right.

Recently there has been some talk of "Constructive Sabotage." Suppose, for example, the workers employed in a candy factory where adulterants were used should go on strike and refuse to use the adulterants, compelling the manufacturer to abandon adulteration and use pure materials. That would be a distinct gain to society, a constructive result. The fallacy here is quite obvious: such a strike is in no sense to be classified as sabotage. Otherwise, all strikes must be regarded as sabotage, and that would rob the word of definite meaning.

Sometimes sabotage takes most amusing forms. In Philadelphia when some tailors went on strike, they are said to have left behind them specially made "yardsticks" a couple of inches short with all the spaces likewise altered. The cutter who cut garments according to his instructions using these false measures was, of course, ruining materials, and one can imagine the most ludicrous results. In Italy, the railroad workers, with fine Italian cunning, suddenly became very "good," and "law-abiding." Not for the world would a railway worker violate the minutest rule. Every rule was most scrupulously obeyed, for the first time in history. The result was the complete demoralization of the system. There were so many rules, many of them long obsolete but never repealed, that any attempt to carry them all out was bound to demoralize the system. When a train started nobody in the entire system could tell where it would end, or how long it would take to reach its destination. The Italian railways became the laughing stock of Europe.

IV.

It will be seen, then, that sabotage is a principle of action rather than a method — a principle of action capable of an almost infinite variety of applications. It may involve violence, or it may be peaceful. It may involve destruction of property or it may not. It may be based on illegal acts or it may not. It may consist of telling lies or of telling the simple truth. It is therefore exceedingly difficult to formulate a satisfactory definition of it, clearly though we may understand its meaning. It is essentially a furtive and stealthy policy, practiced by individual workers, having for its aim the obstruction of industry and business to such an extent that the employers will suffer a loss of profits so great as to be compelled to grant the workers' demands.

It is important that we emphasize the fact that it is essentially a furtive policy practiced by individual workers, though the end sought may be a collective end and the policy may in that sense be called "collective." The restriction of output by labor unions, where the restriction takes the form of a definite maximum rule, is not sabotage. Often such restrictions are expressed in agreements with employers, fixing a definite standard day's work. Such agreements have long been made by some trade unions, and it is utterly foolish to speak of such limitation of output as a form of sabotage, though a great many Syndicalists have done so.

I think that no Syndicalist would include in his definition of sabotage murder, or acts which result in the destruction of human life. Practically every Syndicalist writer insists that such acts do not constitute sabotage. The charge of putting poison in food and candy has been made, but it is probably untrue. Even if it were done it would hardly be fair to call the act one of sabotage. When a great French battleship was blown up and many lives were lost the cry of "Sabotage!" went up all over France. Probably sabotage had nothing to do with it, but if it had the tragic explosion was not contemplated. Otherwise it could not be properly called sabotage, but a terrible act belonging to another category of "direct action." Syndicalists always insist that sabotage is never aimed at human life. To place dynamite under a railroad train or a factory in which people are working, and to cause loss of life is not an act of sabotage.

And yet, it must be confessed that it is well-nigh impossible to wholly separate some forms of sabotage from the destruction of human life. Cutting signal wires on a railway, or placing cement in switches, is likely enough to lead to fatal accidents. So much seems evident. Confusing a railway service would seem to be courting terrible catastrophes and great loss of life. It is a terrible and dangerous game to play at least.

The most amazing thing about the practice of sabotage is the extent to which it can be practiced, the large number of individuals who can participate in a campaign of sabotage. Haywood cites with apparent approval an illustration of this. He is describing the confusion on the French railroads as a result of the mixing up of freight orders, already described, and says:

> "That this was the systematic work of the railroaders there is no question, because a package addressed to Merle one of the editors of *La Guerre Sociale*, now occupying a cell in the Prison of the Saint, was marked with an inscription on the corner 'Sabotagers, please note address.' This package went through post haste."

Then, having made his point, Haywood adds a remark which artlessly exposes a great weakness of the whole policy of sabotage and the manner in which Syndicalism finds itself powerless. He continues:

> "It worked so well that some of the merchants began using the name of *La Guerre Sociale* to have their packages immediately delivered. It was necessary for the managers to threaten to sue them unless they refrained from using the name of the paper for railroad purposes."

What a confession of the weakness of the Syndicalist method this resort to the much-maligned "helpless and impotent State" makes, after all! What a pathetic collapse of the pretentious Syndicalist pride!

V.

I have tried to give a perfectly fair and clear account of sabotage—just what it is, how it is practiced and how it came to be adopted by the Syndicalists as one of their chief weapons. I propose now to set forth with equal plainness the reasons which lead me to reject it root and branch as a weapon of my class. In the autograph album of a visitor to the Socialist Party Convention at Indianapolis I wrote, "Once I believed in sabotage, now I'm against it." Here I shall set forth the reasons for the changed view. I shall write, not as a theorist, but as one having experience. My opposition to sabotage is based upon an intimate personal knowledge.

In the report of MM. Pouget and Delassale to the Toulouse Congress of the *Confédération Générale du Travail*, to which reference has already been made, occurs the following paragraph:

> "The boycott and its indispensable complement, sabotage, furnishes us with an effective means of resistance which — while awaiting the day when the workingmen will be sufficiently strong to emancipate themselves completely — will permit us to stand our ground against the exploitation of which we are the victims."

My own view is that sabotage is not an effective weapon of working class warfare, and that its use can only postpone "the day when the working-men will be sufficiently strong to emancipate themselves completely," and that view I base upon the facts of history. I am not opposed to sabotage because of any love of "law and order," or because of any regard for the "rights of property." None of these things is particularly sacred to me, none of them is one thousandth part as dear to me as the emancipation of my class. If the class to which I belong could be set free from exploitation by violation of the laws made by the master class, by open rebellion, by seizing the property of the rich, by setting the torch to a few buildings, or by the summary execution of a few members of the possessing class, I hope that the courage to share in the work would be mine. I should pray for the courage and the hardness of heart necessary. It is not, then, because of a lack of revolutionary will that I oppose sabotage and the appeal to other violent methods, but because I believe that they can only leave my class more hopelessly enslaved than ever. It is not that I would be careful not to harm the masters of bread and life and to preserve their property, but because I would not destroy the morale of my class as a fighting force.

And that is precisely what sabotage does. It destroys the moral force of the proletariat and unfits it for the great struggle. It weakens the sense of class solidarity already developed. It places the crucial and critical events of the struggle once more in the hands of individuals, not of the mass. When we practiced Ca'Canny in England the employers were at first staggered. They did not know how to deal with such a method of attack, but they soon discovered a way. First came the agents provocateurs, the individuals who came into the unions and urged always violence and more violence. Then came the spies. The unions were beset by all sorts of shady characters. In the seaport where I lived the local branch of the Dockers' Union was full of them. The most active men found themselves on the "blacklist." But that was not all. The spirit of solidarity which had existed was utterly destroyed.

Under the circumstances, it was impossible for the members to trust one another. The consciousness that spies and informers were in the organization led to secretiveness and distrust. Then, too, incriminations and recriminations were rife. The very nature of Ca'Canny invited this. It was so easy to charge that an individual was not in good faith working at reduced speed, but rather "rushing the job"; it was so difficult either to prove or disprove such a charge as to be well-nigh impossible. Within a short time the union was utterly demoralized by internecine strife.

Moreover, Ca'Canny, or sabotage, appeared within the union. Members of the union began to practice Ca'Canny to obtain their own way within the organization. This was a result of our propaganda which had not been foreseen, obvious as it appears in retrospect. Too late, we discovered one of the oldest laws of the psychology of popular movements, the law that the policy adopted in the struggle against the common foe inevitably appears in the internal conflicts of the movement. Teach men and women in the labor movement to practice sabotage in the fight against their employers and it will not be long before they will practice sabotage within their own organizations to obtain factional or personal ends. Union men who practice sabotage against the employer to gain the ends of the union will sooner or later practice sabotage within the union to gain their own ends. A contempt for the will of the majority is developed, for "sabotage is peculiarly the weapon of the rebel minority."

In opposing sabotage, the Socialist Party is opposing that which menaces its own existence as a party of the working class. It is evident to all who have given the matter careful attention that already the Syndicalist element within the party has carried the practice of sabotage inside the party, the obstruction of the work of the party and the impairment of its efficiency, as a party, very far.

At a meeting of the National Executive Committee of the party held in May, 1912, William D. Haywood, a member of the committee and one of the leaders of the I.W.W., declared that one of the chief functions of the latter organization was "the creation of situations for the Socialist Party to meet." He was referring to the "Free Speech" fights of the I.W.W. at San Diego and elsewhere, for which the Socialists were called upon to raise big funds, a task which absorbed a great deal of the party's energy. The significance of the declaration was unmistakable: the I.W.W. was to create critical situations and divert the major part of the energies of the Socialist Party from political action to the work of fighting the battles of the I.W.W. Sabotage within the party could hardly go further than that!

So far I have spoken of those visible evils resulting from sabotage which have come within the sphere of my own observation. There remains yet another danger to be faced, a danger which would seem to be of especial importance to the Syndicalist who looks to the labor union to become the unit of the new social and industrial organization. Can you build a sound and stable structure of rotten materials? In other words, can you first demoralize the workers, train them to work inefficiently and to practice deceit, year after year, possibly for generations, without destroying their capacity for sound citizenship in the new social order? By sabotage the technical efficiency of the producers is impaired, together with their reliance upon collective or mass action in the struggle. Resort to the individual act is given a new sanction at the expense of collective action. Surely, this is weakening the human material of which the Cooperative Commonwealth is to be built!

The most thoughtful of the Syndicalists have seen these dangers most clearly. Men like Sorel and Berth have vigorously opposed sabotage as a reactionary method, destructive of the most hopeful elements in the working class. Thus, Sorel says:

> "Socialism will inherit not only the utensils which have been created by capitalism and the science which has been developed by technical cooperation, but also that power of cooperating which has been developed by a long factory-life in such a way as to get the best out of the time, strength and skill given." He points out that sabotage destroys or greatly impairs this heritage and therefore "does not at all tend to direct the workers in the path of emancipation."

Sabotage is not a weapon of the class-conscious proletariat. Rather is it the weapon of the slum proletariat, "that passively rotting mass thrown off by the lowest layers of old society," to quote Marx, whose conditions of life especially fit it "for the part of a bribed tool of reactionary intrigue." This was clearly shown by Kautsky in a letter published in the New York *Call*. The class-conscious wage-earners, because of their sense of class solidarity, reject the individual struggle against property and depend more and more upon mass action. The master class fears only this mass action, and to head it off sends its agents into the unions to preach individual action in all its forms, including sabotage and riot.

Relation Of Syndicalism To Socialism

I.

The existence of a vigorous Syndicalist agitation is a challenge to the Socialist movement. It inevitably gives rise to certain grave questions which no thoughtful Socialist can ignore or regard with indifference. For example: Is Syndicalism destined to become a permanent part of the revolutionary movement of the proletariat, or is it merely a temporary phase of the development of the movement? — Is it likely to make a successful appeal to the organized proletariat of those nations in which the class consciousness of the workers is most developed and the working-class organization the most advanced? — Will the success of Syndicalism hasten or retard the realization of the Socialist ideal? — What attitude must the Socialist political movement adopt toward the Syndicalist agitation?

Obviously, such questions as these are not to be categorically disposed of. Dogmatic replies to most questions of this sort are as vain as indifference to them. Our best and profoundest answers to most of the foregoing questions must be conditional and not absolute. It would be foolish to deny the possibility of Syndicalism becoming a fixed and permanent form of proletarian warfare, for instance, though our most candid and serious investigation and study may lead us to believe it improbable and to expect the Syndicalist agitation to lose its aggressiveness and become merged in the general proletarian struggle. History is full of warnings against the futility and folly of dogmatism upon questions to which only the test of Time can give reliable and authentic answers. Bismarck declared that the Socialist movement could never take root and flourish in the political and intellectual life of Germany. Gladstone made a similar declaration concerning the impossibility of Socialism in England. Each regarded as a whim, a temporary phase of popular temper, what has become the most vital force in the life of two great modern nations. The nonconformity of the Wesleys and their co-laborers was likewise regarded as a mere temporary aberration, but, like Socialism, it assumed a permanent place in the life of the world.

And yet, those who expect to see the tide of Syndicalist agitation subside have on their side the witness of history to the fact that Syndicalism is in all respects similar to numerous storms of popular agitation which, at various times, have arisen to alarm the world and then gradually subsided. As we have seen, the specific doctrines of the Syndicalists have been made the basis of great agitations at various times during the past eighty years, beginning with Robert Owen. And its particular and distinctive methods, its contempt for parliamentary efforts and its reliance upon strikes, insurrections and other forms of "direct action" are just as old, and have appeared just as often. There is nothing in the present Syndicalist agitation to suggest that it is likely to be more permanent than any of its predecessors; there is no phase of Syndicalism today that is new, upon which one might base either the hope or the unwilling belief that at last the ideals and methods of Robert Owen, Pierre J. Proudhon, Feargus O'Connor and Michael

Bakunin have become firmly rooted in the proletarian movement.

I know that there are some who think that the basis for such a hope or belief is afforded by the tremendous strength of the present day Syndicalist movement, the number of those who shout its shibboleths and avow their belief in its principles and practices. For such a view history offers no support whatever. Those who are thus impressed by the numerical strength of the present agitation must be unfamiliar with the history of similar movements of the past. They must be unfamiliar with the fact that, having regard to the time, the essential principles of modern Syndicalism have a much smaller following today than they had four score years ago or than they had sixty-five years ago. Nowhere in the world today, so far as I know, have the Syndicalists anything like the following that Owen had in 1834 or that the Chartists had in 1842 and 1848. Of course, it may be objected that Chartism was primarily a movement to obtain the franchise and other political rights, not an economic movement like Syndicalism. To some extent, that objection is justified. It cannot be urged against Owenism, however, which was in all respects identical with the Syndicalism of today. And even the Chartist movement was at bottom a movement for economic emancipation. Moreover, from 1839 to its collapse in 1849 its chief policies were identical with the main policies of modern Syndicalism.

Exaggeration of the strength of popular movements is common and universal. The clamorous agitation in which they must indulge, and the excitement they create, lead to this. Bernard Shaw has told in an amusing way how a few Socialist journalists in England in the early eighteen-eighties convinced a great part of the British public that a formidable movement was already menacing the existing social order, when in fact there were very few Socialists in England. The strength of the International Workingmen's Association was likewise vastly overestimated. So it is with Syndicalism. No real measure of its strength seems possible at present, but we do know that only a very small minority of the workers, even in France, can be said to be intelligently and definitely committed to the policies of revolutionary Syndicalism. The *Confédération Générale du Travail* embraces little more than half of the labor unions of France, and its total membership is far less than one-half of the total number of organized workers.In 1910 there were 5,260 labor unions in France, 3,012 of which were in the *Confédération*. There were 977,350 organized workers of which only 357,814 belonged to the *Confédération*. The total number of organized workers is a pitiful minority of the working class, and of that minority the *Confédération* is itself a minority.

And that minority, the *Confédération*, is not by any means solid in its adherence to the revolutionary ideals and policies which we have outlined and discussed. It is well-known that a minority of the members of the *Confédération* determine its policies. The *Confédération* is made up of a large number of very small local unions, some federations of local unions, and the *Bourses du Travail*, or labor exchanges, which are found in nearly all cities and supported by subsidies from municipal funds. Now, each constituent member of the *Confédération* has one vote and one only. Thus a small group of Anarchists can form a local union, join the *Confédération* and exercise just as much electoral power in the organization as a big union of hundreds of members. At the Marseilles Congress, in 1908, the glovemakers were represented by five unions claiming a total membership of 500 members. Therefore they had five votes for 500 members. But the miners were represented by thirty-five unions claiming a total membership of 140,000, and had accordingly thirty-five votes. The building trades also claimed 40,000 members, but had 336 unions and as many votes. So long as these conditions prevail the determined minority, composed largely of Anarchists, will rule. It is unlikely, however, that the large unions will permit the small unions to exert this undue influence in the organization very much longer. Once that system is replaced by a system of proportional representation the labor movement in France will, in all probability, enter upon a phase of development analogous to that which has characterized the British and German movements, and draw much closer to the political Socialist movement. Of course, the Syndicalists are bitterly opposed to all forms of proportional representation, as they are to democracy in general.

For the reasons already given, and the further reason that all labor movements, born as they are in times of conflict and oppression, begin with extremely radical tendencies and become more and more opportunistic as they develop strength, I have reached the conclusion that the Syndicalist movement will either pass away, its main theories and policies becoming the subject of periodical agitation, or will be greatly modified, until its present distinctive characteristics which alienate it from the rest of the working-class movement are given up, and it becomes part and parcel of the great movement struggling equally on the political and economic fields.

II.

Sweeping generalizations concerning the relation of national temperaments to a movement like Syndicalism are easily made, and as treacherous as they are easy. It is easy to ascribe Syndicalism to the special temperament of the people of France, Italy and Spain, the three countries in which it has acquired its greatest strength. Such a psychological explanation overlooks the fact that, at times not remote, it has appealed equally to the English mind and acquired great strength while the rest of the world was, on the whole, indifferent to it. Today the British worker is little influenced by Syndicalism. Are we to ascribe this change to at corresponding change in those fundamental qualities of mind and spirit which we call "temperament," or to a changed viewpoint which reflects great changes in actual conditions? The Germany of 1848 and the England of 1848 were not less revolutionary— using that word in the popular sense— than was the France of 1848. The *Marseillaise* was as popular in

London and Manchester, Berlin and Cologne as it was in Paris or Lyons. "Bread or Revolution!" was the cry in England. "To arms! To the barricades!" was the cry in Germany. If nowadays these excitements are less common in Germany and England than in France, Italy, Spain and the South American Republics, it is not due to "temperament," but to the fact that in Germany and England conditions due to industrial development, and the experience of more than sixty years, have led to a general abandonment of the ancient methods of revolutionary action in favor of methods which demand greater self-discipline and restraint and better organization.

What is frequently spoken of as the incitement of French and Italian temperament is in reality a limitation imposed by the weakness of the proletariat in those countries; their lack of effective organization. What is regarded as daring is in reality very often mere desperation. Of course, the French and Italian Syndicalists use their "temperament" to hide their weakness. "We have no organization, but we have a temperament," they say. At the International Congress at Stuttgart, in 1907, Karl Legien, the leader of the German trade unions, brusquely swept this little vanity aside and declared: "It is not with temperament that one fights the employer. As soon as the French have an actual trade union organization they will cease discussing blindly the General Strike, direct action and sabotage."

Greulich, the heroic veteran of Switzerland, so long the friend of Marx, pointed to the same lesson, that direct action in general and the General Strike in particular are methods which belong to the period of infantile weakness:

> "Where the unions have acquired a sure power and a certain vitality, the General Strike is considered by the workers as a Utopia.

> "The General Strike is a childish fancy of poorly organized workers. The English workers lived in this dream from about 1830-1840, and they made many times remarkable attempts to realize this dream — attempts compared with

which the 'General Strike' of today is but child's play. They covered entire industrial centers, and stopped work in all the factories and mines. The revolutionary energy was not lacking in them, where they met with resistance: they besieged factories and set fire to them; they fought valiantly with police and the military. And if the General Strike had been really a decisive power, England would not have had enough soldiers to render herself the master."

Here in America the Syndicalism of the I.W.W. makes its greatest progress among that section of our proletariat which has not yet acquired the franchise, and which hails from those European countries in which the labor movement is weak. Their conception of revolutionary action is primitive and undeveloped. They are French, Italian, Spanish or Swiss, seeing things from the viewpoint of their respective nationalities. Let them acquire citizenship, a larger knowledge of our institutions and the control which through them the proletariat may exercise over the economic organization of society, and they will be largely lost to the I.W.W., or will effectually modify its policies.

In a word, the Syndicalist movement is Utopian; its aim and the methods of attaining its realization do not correspond to the realities of modern industrial and political life but are deductions from abstract principles. In countries where, as in France, Italy and Spain, industrialism is a full century behind, the Syndicalist movement can maintain a greater degree of vigor and virility than would be possible in England, Germany or America. But let the industrial development of France, Italy, Spain or similar countries be accelerated as was that of Germany after 1871 and, as an inevitable consequence, the labor movement in those countries will develop better and more stable forms of organization, not dependent upon temperament but upon power and discipline and material resources. What seems to me to be the logical interpretation of the history of modem proletarian movements is that Syndicalism is dangerous, not because it has any chance of becoming the dominant form of labor organization in those nations in which the class consciousness of the workers is most developed and the working-class organization the most advanced, but because it is likely to be the means of maintaining a division in the fighting force of the proletariat and weakening it in the struggle to achieve its emancipation.

III.

Even if the Syndicalist movement could completely achieve its goal, its triumph would not be at all the realization of the Socialist ideal. Ownership and control of the industries by the workers actually engaged in them is a very different ideal from the socialization of industry, its ownership and control by society democratically organized. Whether we think of the ownership and control of all industry by one vast union of workers with centralized authority, or of a series of local industrial unions owning and controlling local industries, it is difficult to see how an industrial hierarchy is to be avoided, the workers occupying strategic positions in the industrial organism becoming a privileged class. Are there not large social interests involved in all industry, or nearly all, which the workers cannot be expected, as workers, to adequately guard? The workers engaged in transportation, for example, can have no claim to the exclusive control of the means of transportation. The citizens as a whole have vastly important interests at stake, interests which cannot be safeguarded except by the representation of the community as such in the management. No amount of quibbling, it seems to me, can hide the fact that the present Syndicalist ideal falls far short of the Socialist ideal in its recognition of our ever-increasing interdependence.

Let us suppose, however, that this difficulty, which the Syndicalists have nowhere treated with the seriousness its importance deserves, could be satisfactorily surmounted; let us even grant that the Syndicalists would so manage industry as to obviate every difficulty and do exact justice to all, there would remain still problems of infinite importance, not arising from the management of industry but from the mere association of people in particular areas, in other words, vast social problems for the solution of which industrial capacity—even admitting the unions to possess a monopoly of that—is in no sense a preparation.

Of course, the assumption that the labor union is by its very nature the proper unit of social government and administration is itself open to the most serious question. What preparation does labor union activity afford for such an important role? To be absolutely candid about it, the very nature of the labor union, the work it must perform in present society, tends to unfit it for the part the Syndicalists would impose upon it. Its work is critical and destructive. It does not concern itself with the constructive work of industrial organization and management. It is in this respect very different from the cooperative association which actually deals with the problems of the efficient organization and management of industry. If experience and preparation mean anything at all, the cooperative associations are far better fitted to assume the management and direction of actual industry than are the labor unions.

But, let us not press these unsolved problems of Syndicalism home with too much emphasis. We must bear in mind that Syndicalist speculations concerning the social organization of the future, like similar speculations by Socialists, are not to be regarded too seriously. As in all forecasts, there is the great element of individual desire, a factor which the realities of social evolution will treat with scant respect. Even if the Syndicalist should ultimately be vindicated in so far that the labor union of to-day assumes a new function and becomes the unit of the social and economic organization of a new society, the germ of the ideal commonwealth, which seems to me to be most unlikely, it is probable that social safeguards, limitations of power, checks now undreamed of will be devised to conserve the social interests.

There is yet another sense in which, as I see it, the Syndicalist movement is bound to stop far short of the Socialist goal. The emphasis it places upon the strike and upon economic gains as opposed to social gains achieved by legislation, dooms the movement to what may be termed economic opportunism. Unless I am greatly mistaken, the I.W.W. in this country is already weakened by this inevitable tendency to economic opportunism. Each strike won, though the gain be only a few cents a week, or a trivial shortening of hours, is hailed as a great "victory" and an inspiration to struggle for further "victories" elsewhere. By an irresistible process the movement uses its victories as tests of its growth; they become its criteria. The ultimate goal is lost sight of, or at least obscured. Just as political opportunism, against which the Syndicalist rails, leads to the glorification of electoral success, so that to obtain and hold parliamentary power becomes an immediate purpose so vast as to obscure the goal, the means becoming the end, so the economic opportunism which threatens Syndicalism, leads to the over emphasis of wage increases and forgetfulness of the original purpose, the destruction of the wage system itself. If it be true that a party which pins its faith to reform legislation, and devotes its energies to passing such legislation, becomes a party of reform, degenerates and loses its revolutionary temper, it is equally true that a movement which pins its faith to economic action, and devotes its energies to securing immediate material gains by means of such action, tends to become wholly occupied with immediate ends and to lose sight of the revolutionary goal. Upon this rock the great economic movements of the past have split. The tendency of Syndicalism to degenerate to the level of the most conservative labor unionism will, I predict, become more and more marked with every successful strike.

IV.

What, then, should be the Socialist attitude toward Syndicalism? That question can best be answered by setting forth the position of the great international Socialist movement and comparing it with the position of the Syndicalists. Perhaps no better statement of the Socialist position was ever made than the brief declaration of principles adopted by the International Socialist Congress at Paris, in 1900, with practical unanimity, only one vote being cast against it. The statement reads:

> "The modem proletariat is a necessary result of the capitalist organization of production. For the capitalist organization of production depends on having an object for exploitation, and it finds this in the enslaved working class, without economic or political independence. The liberation of this class can come only in opposition to those who support the capitalist organization of production (which, by the way, from its own inherent characteristics, is tending toward the socialization of production). Consequently, there is but one course open to the proletariat, and that is, as a class, to oppose the capitalists.

> "Social Democracy has taken upon itself the task of organizing the proletariat into an army ready for the social war, and it must, therefore, above all else, ensure that the working classes become conscious of their class interests and of their strength. To this end it must adopt every possible measure, and advocate every possible reform. In particular, the Congress would suggest participation in political life, the demand for universal suffrage, the organization of the working classes in political, trade union and cooperative groups, workingmen's educational societies, and so forth.

> "The Congress calls upon Socialists in all countries to see to it that all these forms, at one and the same time educational agencies and weapons for the fight, shall everywhere work together hand-in-hand. In this way, the power of the working classes will gradually grow, until eventually it will

be enabled to deprive the middle classes of their economic and political influence, and to socialize the means of production."

This statement makes clear what I venture to call the four cardinal points of Socialist policy, to wit:

1.   The goal toward which we strive is the socialization of the instruments of production and the abolition of class rule.

2.   The inherent characteristics of capitalist production force it in the direction of the goal.

3.   Nevertheless, the realization of the goal can only come as a result of the conscious warfare of the proletariat.

4.   The struggle of the proletariat must comprehend three methods — political action, that is, parliamentary action, trade unionism and cooperation.

It is quite evident that the Socialist movement cannot be limited to parliamentary action alone. There may have been at one period a disposition to advocate political action only and to belittle and discourage trade unionism and cooperation, but that attitude is no longer much in evidence anywhere. The great growth of trade unionism and cooperation in the leading industrial countries has brought the movement the practical assurance that these forms of action do not limit or weaken the political struggle, but greatly strengthen it. The three methods admirably supplement each other and the Socialist movement is most successful in those countries in which the three are blended.

But, while the Socialist movement is not merely political and parliamentary, it is of necessity a political and parliamentary movement. Everywhere the recognized policy of the Socialist movement emphasizes participation in parliamentary and political action as the primary need and duty of the working class. That was settled at the International Congress held at Zurich, in 1893, when a resolution was passed making "participation in legislation and parliamentary activity" a condition of eligibility to representation at all future congresses, a condition of equal importance with the belief in "social ownership and socialized production." The resolution declares that only those may participate in the congresses of the international movement who can meet the following conditions:

> "1. Representatives of all bodies that are striving to replace the capitalist order of private ownership and private production by social ownership and socialized production, and that look upon participation in legislation and parliamentary activity as necessary means to achieve that end.

> "2. All trade union organizations which, although they may not themselves take part in the political struggle, yet realize the necessity of that struggle. Anarchists are thus excluded."

At the London Congress in 1896 a vigorous attempt was made to rescind this resolution and to seat the Anarchists. A great deal was made of the "intolerance" of the position taken at Zurich. The Anarchists were excluded, however, and since that time the matter has been regarded as settled. There is hardly a dissenting voice raised in the movement nowadays against the continuance of the policy established by the Zurich and London Congresses. Scant attention would be paid today to any demand for the readmission of the Anarchists. Naturally, what applies to the international congresses applies equally to the national movements themselves; the profession of Anarchist opinions, disbelief in political action in the parliamentary sense of that term, disqualifies the person holding such views from being a member of the Socialist Party in any country.

Our position toward the Anarchists is necessarily one of unrelenting hostility and open warfare. It is a fundamental article of our Socialist faith that the proletariat must participate in legislation and parliamentary activity in order to emancipate itself. The Anarchist wants merely to destroy the power of the State, while the Socialist wants to acquire that power and use it.

Now, it does not matter that the Anarchist label is removed from the characteristic policies of Anarchism and a new label attached to them. Antagonism to parliamentary action is the same anti-Socialist policy whether labeled Anarchist or Syndicalist. Exclusive reliance upon "direct action" is the same evil from our point of view whether urged by a Malatesta or a John Most in the name of Anarchism, by a Labriola or a Lagardelle in the name of Syndicalism or by a Haywood or a Trautman in the name of the Industrial Workers of the World. Whatever philosophical elements the Syndicalist movement contains which are foreign to Anarchism, one thing is quite certain, namely, that its practical policies are purely Anarchistic and anti-Socialist.

The existence of the Socialist Party is menaced by the presence within its ranks of fundamentally antagonistic elements, whose propaganda for direct action and against parliamentary action and legislation is more dangerous to it than any of the forces which are arrayed against it on the outside. There are some words of Wilhelm Liebknecht, uttered as a warning against political compromises for the sake of vote-getting, which seem to me to apply with equal force to the dangers of compromise with Anarchistic schismatics for the sake of a delusive formal "unity" and a mistaken " tolerance."

> "The enemy who comes to us with open visor we face with a smile; to set our feet upon his neck is mere play for us. The stupidly brutal acts of violence of police politicians, the outrages of anti-Socialist laws, penitentiary bills — these only arouse feelings of pitying contempt; the enemy, however, that reaches out the hand to us for a political alliance, and intrudes himself upon us as a friend and a brother, him and him alone have we to fear.

> "Our fortress can withstand every assault—it cannot be stormed nor taken from us by siege— it can only fall when we ourselves open the door: to the enemy and take him into our ranks as a fellow comrade."

As I see it, then, there is just as much danger to the Socialist movement in a compromise with Anarchism in its Syndicalist guise as in a compromise with capitalistic political parties. In either case, we sell our birthright for a miserable mess of pottage. Not only is it our right as Socialists to demand an unqualified acceptance of the principle of political action as a condition of membership in the Socialist movement, but that is also our duty, unpleasant though it may at times become. Nor can we accept equivocal phrases and permit men to belong to our organization just because they are willing to affirm belief in "political action," when we know that by political action they mean something quite other than the term means to us. To paralyze government by means of a great strike or uprising is frequently the conception, and the only conception, covered by the term "political action" as used by our shamefaced Syndicalist friends. Of course, that is the merest subterfuge. By political action we mean, in the language of the National Constitution of the Socialist Party, "participation in elections for public office and practical legislative and administrative work along the lines of the Socialist Party platform." Only those who can give loyal and unequivocal assent to political action so defined can have any rational claim to a place in the Socialist ranks.

Yet it would be folly of the worst type to suppose that mere exclusion of the Syndicalists from the party ranks will solve the problem. That is a necessary step, but it is only a step. It is more important still to exclude the causes of the despair of political action which breeds Syndicalism. That which leads more than anything else to the development of Syndicalist tendencies in the political movement is that form of political opportunism which in its eagerness for immediate reforms, or for electoral power, loses the revolutionary vision and with it the revolutionary temper and aim.

To be at once vigorous and faithful in the pursuit of the revolutionary goal and effective in the present struggle for immediate gains, that is the ideal which the political Socialist movement must set before itself and strive to realize. Too often, as in the case of the British Labor Party, for example, political opportunism leads to a policy of mere reform. Perhaps, after all, the greatest antidote to Syndicalism will be found to be the infusion of the political Socialist movement with greater daring. Better a small parliamentary group which dares to light than a large parliamentary delegation which is anxious most of all to maintain its reputation for sobriety of judgment, practicality and sweet reasonableness. If the Syndicalist agitation leads to the inspiration of the Socialist parties of the world with a larger audacity, without destroying the patience and capacity to wage the immediate struggle for reform, it will have done much to condone the evil it has wrought.

For the Socialist in politics a degree of audacity and daring that is almost sublime is essential. His motto might well be the historic saying of Danton, *De l'audace, encore de l'audace, et tonjours de l'audace!*

www.ingramcontent.com/pod-product-compliance
Lightning Source LLC
Chambersburg PA
CBHW060908280326
41934CB00007B/1239